D1648954

THE ROW 34 COOKBOOK

THE ROW 34 COOKBOOK

Stories and Recipes from a Neighborhood Oyster Bar

Jeremy Sewall with
Erin Byers Murray

Photography by
Michael Harlan Turkell

RIZZOLI
NEW YORK

New York Paris London Milan

I would like to dedicate this book to the past, present, and future Row 34 employees.

Their hard work and dedication are a symbol of all that I love about this business.

—Jeremy Sewall

Contents

Foreword

by Renee Erickson, chef and owner, The Walrus and the Carpenter, The Whale Wins, Barnacle, Bar Melusine, Bateau, Westward, General Porpoise Doughnuts and Coffee, and Willmott's Ghost

I'll never forget the first road trip Jeremy Sewall and I took together to visit Hama Hama Oysters on the Hood Canal in Washington. A visit to the beloved farm, a sanctuary of dear friends and bivalves for me for many years, was to be a new West Coast adventure for Jeremy and his team. As we drove toward the canal, zipping past fir trees, I realized he'd be a lifelong friend. Stuffed into the back seat of my midsize SUV with his colleague and my 110-pound pup, Mr. Arlo, Jeremy put us all at ease with his silly dog talk and spoke of his love for oysters, clams, and anything that came out of the sea.

To love oysters as much as we both do is a bit out of the ordinary in the modern chef world. Many restaurants sell oysters on the half shell, but usually the person preparing them is hidden away and the position is filled by a young cook who is not only learning how to dress the perfect salad and set pâté, but is also charged with shucking a dozen gnarly oysters in a hurry. It's safe to say that it's rarely done well.

Jeremy and I take a different approach, which is less hidden, more center stage. The first thing that hits you when you step onto a quality oyster farm, like Island Creek Oysters in Duxbury, Massachusetts, or Hama Hama on the Hood Canal, is the smell of the sea. To honor that essential detail, we've put shucking stations front and center in our restaurants, right as you walk in the door. They're a showcase of beauty, craft, and the intoxicating aroma of the sea. Every time I walk into my oyster bar, The Walrus and the Carpenter in the Ballard neighborhood of Seattle, or his stunning Row 34 oyster bar in the historic Fort Point neighborhood in Boston, I'm exhilarated. There is no other food in the world that makes me this happy.

Reading Jeremy's book, I'm reminded of the first time I ate a fried clam. In the Northwest we don't fry our clams; we craft clam soups and stews. So, this was new and delightful to me. Yes, both Seattle and Boston cuisines are heavily influenced by what we catch in the surrounding waters, but the history and cookery behind them are very different. Jeremy and I have similar cooking styles: a simple, ingredient-driven method that is often overlooked or underutilized in today's kitchens. Jeremy has spent more than two decades honing his skills with ingredients and styles that are a part of his family history and that honor New England in an honest, straightforward way.

It's no surprise, then, that the recipes in this book have been developed, tested, eaten, and perfected over lifetimes in the Northeast. It's the kind of food that has been passed down from families and fishermen for generations. Not only has Jeremy written recipes you will want to make every Sunday, but he tells the story of oysters, farmers, fishermen, lobstermen, and New England that makes me dream of times past. Meals from a simpler era, like New England clam chowder, corn pancakes with smoked salmon, and probably the most valuable of them all (and my favorite), Grandma Ethel's classic lobster roll. Grandmas are truly the best. Food like this makes us strong and durable. It gives us hope and connection to our homes—something we all very much need in life.

To love food is to take comfort in what is to come. It's the excitement and impatience of a meal on the horizon. For me, it is also knowing that my friend Jeremy is on the other coast planning an upcoming meal that teaches the next generation of cooks and eaters what it is to truly love seafood. Right now, it's a cold and rainy day here in Seattle as I sit looking out the window planning for my next tray of cold, crisp oysters and a cool glass of muscadet. I imagine that Jeremy is doing the same thing . . . only with a beer instead.

Introduction

At the start of creating this book, which now seems like a lifetime ago, I was at an amazing place in my career. I had multiple successful restaurants, I was thinking about opening more, and I was loving it all. And then, well, COVID-19 turned all of our worlds upside down overnight. Few industries were hit as hard as the restaurant and hospitality industry.

Now, as I sit down to write this, we're months into it. And I'm not sure that all of my restaurants will survive. Those that do will continue with the mission of serving beautiful food and offering warm, inviting hospitality. How and when this industry, or even just segments of it, come back to life is still uncertain. Restaurants, chefs, farmers, fishermen and women, and all who participate in the process are not going away, but the way they all interact with one another will certainly change.

I've now learned what I should have already known: Value every guest, run an efficient kitchen, and most of all, food is a precious gift that we miss when we can't or don't have access to it. Personally, I miss my life with food. Ordering beautiful products from farmers and fishermen; creating menu descriptions; training the staff; and celebrating the entire process by putting all of that on a plate and serving it to a guest in the restaurant. Many of us have had to put that life on pause. But I've learned that my love for food goes far beyond what happens in a restaurant. I've found great joy in cooking for my family and neighbors, in feeding those I love. It's been a moment I might never have had otherwise.

None of this changes the history of Row 34. But it might change its future. I am not sure where the story of Row 34 will be headed by the time you read this, but I remain hopeful that it's a story that will continue for a long time to come.

Row 34, Boston and Portsmouth

Fort Point is a sliver of land that touches South Boston and the Seaport District and overlooks the Financial District across the Congress Street Bridge. It's one of those corners of the city that easily connects to most other parts of downtown. Originally, a hill sat on this jut of land, and that's where a battery of cannons was set up during colonial times to protect the inner harbor of Boston. It's a short distance from where the actual Boston Tea Party took place. Much later, in the 1830s, the land was leveled, and the surrounding wetlands were filled in, which is when the Fort Point neighborhood began to take shape. The Boston Wharf Company constructed a number of warehouses and factories here, since the area was easily accessible to the waterfront. Toward the 1930s, Fort Point became a center for the wool trade in America. We believe that the building that is now Row 34 was once home to a wool and textile storage facility. Its last commercial use was for steel storage during World War II.

After warehousing and manufacturing declined in the twentieth century, the area became home to the largest community of artists in New England. In the 1970s, it was a hub and refuge where artists worked and lived. There is still a large artist community that occupies Fort Point.

As the rest of Boston started to see redevelopment, many of the neighborhood buildings in Fort Point became rundown—Fort Point was almost forgotten. Then, in 2004, a developer named Young Park bought thirteen buildings and lots in the area with the vision of transforming the neighborhood into a distinct part of the city that could be preserved without losing its identity. Part of the allure was the distinctive architecture—uniform-looking, side-by-side brick-front loft buildings—which made Fort Point feel like a unique part of the Boston landscape.

When we first stepped into the building on the corner of Congress Street and Boston Wharf Road, it was hard to imagine what it might become. Built in 1907, it had been empty for quite some time, though a few resident artists remained. The building was brought down to its brick shell, and inside, we discovered amazing northwestern redwood beams, which we kept. Everything else was gutted. The exterior remains intact. We wanted to retain that character, especially since it fits so beautifully with the surrounding buildings.

Standing in the space for the first time, I couldn't imagine how it would become a fully functioning restaurant. (There would also be residential units constructed above the restaurant.) Watching the transformation from completely raw space with a dirt floor into a vibrant restaurant was unforgettable for me.

This became the home of our first Row 34. It was the second oyster bar that my partners and I opened. Island Creek Oyster Bar in Kenmore Square was the first. Island Creek connected a local oyster farm and the people behind it with a city restaurant. Skip Bennett, the founder and owner of the farm Island Creek Oysters, had already turned Duxbury, Massachusetts, into an oyster mecca and was doing the work of transforming the oyster business. I feel lucky to have been able to do this with Skip—a chef and an oyster farmer opening a restaurant together. The second restaurant was meant to be smaller and less formal. Well, we got less formal but not necessarily smaller. The "everyday" oyster bar opened in November 2013.

The Name

We named Row 34 after an oyster Skip had started growing in Duxbury using a method that was new to him and involved loving and touching the oysters often during the growing process. They were flipped regularly to help develop a deep cup and they did not grow as large as the traditional Island Creek oysters. Most cultivated oysters spend some time in a rack-and-bag system set off the bottom of the bay floor. This type of system is lined up in rows like a vineyard. (All of Skip's Island Creek oysters spend at least some of their oyster lives in this type of system, but most are then placed on the bottom of Duxbury Bay to finish growing.) When Skip started trying the then-new method, he put the oysters nurtured in this novel way in the thirty-fourth row of his system. And that's how we got the name.

In the early days, writing the menu at Row 34 was very stressful for me for some reason. I came up with the idea that we would print a new menu daily. We attempt to use the best of what is local, with oysters, lobsters, and beyond, and it forced us to remain nimble. Boats don't get out to fish every day and don't always catch the fish you want to cook. So, I write the menu backward: I find the ingredients and then write the menu.

We started with what we thought of as the core of what a Fort Point oyster bar should have: an epic oyster program; lobster rolls; fried clams; a great burger. But then I got a little stuck. Sourcing seafood is a ridiculous infatuation for me, and I didn't want having another restaurant to change that. At the time, I had my own little refrigerated truck. Mostly, I drove myself up to Maine to pick up lobsters or to the Boston fish pier to buy my fish, because in my opinion, that is the very best way to source seafood. It's hard as a chef to not overthink a menu—but you also don't want to lose the true identity of your food, and you strive to work with it the way it's intended to be used. So, we started with what we had: access to great seafood.

I wanted the raw bar menu to be pretty straightforward, so we focused on New England–grown oysters; after all, we have access to some of the best around. Island Creek oysters, of course, and Skip's Row 34s in particular quickly became our guests' favorites. The quality and variety of oysters produced in New England is continually improving, which gives us great options to fill our list. We developed a ceviche and crudo program next, and then we added our smoked and cured dishes. This is one of my favorite parts of the menu. It gives me the opportunity to be creative and I've developed a few items that have become staples for the restaurant: smoked scallops, bluefish pâté, smoked oysters and mussels, cured mackerel. They all became a way to showcase seafood differently for people, and in a way that I had only done in small doses before. From there, the regular menu finally started to take shape. Beer-steamed mussels. Grilled whole fish. Pasta with littlenecks. Roasted haddock. Francisco's deviled crab toast. That's when the menu started to flow.

The most important thing in those early days was (and still is) executing it all correctly. Beautifully shucked oysters, seafood that is cooked with purpose, balanced flavors, and a kitchen team that is thoughtful in their approach. All of this, plus a crew of enthusiastic staffers, brought Row 34 to life.

Expanding to Portsmouth

A couple years into Row 34's life, we were anxious to build on the success we'd created in Fort Point. We ventured to Portsmouth, New Hampshire, to try our hand at it again. Portsmouth is a lovely small town on the seacoast with a great restaurant community and a growing family of oyster farmers nearby. My own family is from just over the Piscataqua River in Kittery and York, Maine. I was very familiar with Portsmouth and felt like it could be a great place for another Row. We found local farmers, fishermen, and aquaculturists, and today, we celebrate them on our menu, just as we do in Boston. Although this restaurant is in a newer building and we don't have the grandness of the Fort Point space, Row 34 Portsmouth has become its own defined space that, just like the Boston location, feels like it fits right in. We've become that neighborhood oyster bar once again.

Not much has changed from those early days. Oysters, especially when eaten from a big communal platter, are fun, and people enjoy their experience when they come in. People love the beer program and the space. Outside our doors, a lot is happening to the neighborhood of Fort Point. Congress Street feels the same, but as I look out the front door toward the Seaport, the horizon is dramatically different. Buildings are going up all the time and the area that sits right next to Fort Point is one of the busiest in Boston these days. It's a big change from the first time I stepped foot in Fort Point. But all of what I first fell in love with about the area is still intact. As much as things change around it, Fort Point continues to be a tiny sliver of land where history remains, and its identity stays the same. And that's exactly what we want for Row 34, too.

How to Use This Cookbook

I want you to cook and eat seafood—I really do. This cookbook is meant to help reduce some of the challenges, or perceived challenges, that come with cooking seafood.

The recipes are either pulled directly from my restaurant kitchens and adapted for home cooks, or they are for dishes I cook in my own home kitchen. They are meant to make it possible for everyone to enjoy well-prepared seafood at home. Don't let little obstacles stop you from cooking a dish. Be ready to substitute fish species, alter ingredients, and make small adjustments as you go.

The more comfortable you become with cooking seafood, the easier it will be to find preparations and flavors that you love, and you can build on those as long as you enjoy cooking. Be excited to try new things; seafood offers endless possibilities for new dishes. Start here with some basics and enjoy the journey.

Handling and Storing

Always treat seafood delicately. Don't store anything on top of the seafood and keep it cold and dry until ready to use. Cradle filets and whole fish gently. Shellfish can crack, so be careful not to bang them around.

Don't store fish or shellfish in fresh water. If you place seafood on top of ice, make sure to remove the seafood as the ice melts so that it's not sitting in water. *Note: Your fishmonger should be handling fish the same way.*

Cooking Equipment and General Pointers

• A basic fish spatula is a great investment; you will find it indispensable with these recipes.

• I like to sauté fish in a heavy stainless steel pan or a cast-iron pan. If you are new to pan-searing fish, a nonstick pan is a good place to start.

• Don't use tongs on a piece of fish unless it has bones in it. Using tongs to move tails and collars on a grill is fine, but those same tongs will tear filets apart in a pan or on a grill.

• Use a cake tester to check fish for doneness. If you poke a piece of cooked fish with a cake tester, you can tell how well done it is from the resistance: more resistance means the fish is barely cooked through; less resistance means it is cooked through.

• Pay attention to the thickness or size of a piece of fish, since that might make it necessary to adjust your cooking times. Always check before serving to make sure that it is cooked to the desired doneness.

Seasoning

• Acid and salt are your best friends when seasoning seafood.

• I use Diamond Crystal kosher salt in all my recipes. If you don't have access to that brand, at least make sure you're using kosher salt.

• White pepper, when used with restraint, adds a nice flavor; black pepper is a stronger flavor. I like white pepper for some of my seafood dishes and often call for freshly ground black pepper. Throughout the cookbook you'll read, "season with salt and pepper." Remember to use pepper with restraint, as it can overpower some seafood.

• Always use freshly squeezed citrus; it makes a difference.

• High-quality vinegars are great with certain seafoods, and there are more and more small-batch vinegars on the market now. Use vinegar to season dishes or sprinkle over seafood just before serving. But remember, restraint is important.

• Taste and season as you go. When cooking with dried spices, you want to accent or highlight the seafood you are preparing, not overwhelm it.

Frying Seafood at Home

Fried fish can taste amazing when prepared correctly. While fried food has a reputation of being greasy or heavy, it doesn't have to be.

• Work with dry food. Water and moisture make frying more difficult and can be dangerous. Let ingredients such as potatoes and vegetables drain well before frying, and pat them dry with paper towels.

• My go-to oil for frying is canola. It holds up well and has a neutral flavor. Vegetable, soybean, corn, and peanut oils are also good to use.

• Clean oil makes a big difference in the final product. You can strain oil after each use and use it again one or two more times. But when you can't see the bottom of the pan or fryer through the oil, that means it's time to change the oil.

• Deep frying is when the product is completely surrounded by or submerged in oil. When deep frying, it is important not to overload the oil,

which will make the oil's temperature decrease rapidly—that's when you end up with "greasy" fried food.

• It's usually best to fry in smaller batches. Otherwise, if the pan is crowded, the pieces will not cook evenly.

• When panfrying, make sure the oil is deep enough to go about halfway up the side of the item being fried. The goal is to get the item crispy on one side and cooked about 70 percent of the way through. Flip and finish cooking on the other side.

• I recommend buying a countertop deep fryer that can hold 3 quarts to 1 gallon of oil. Most models have a thermostat that is easy to control and will hold the temperature of the oil.

• If you don't have a deep fryer, the next best tool is a Dutch oven. Use a thermometer to make sure the oil is the correct temperature.

• Always be careful when frying. The fryer should be in a secure place. Let the oil cool completely before moving. Always prepare a paper towel–lined plate or pan in advance so it is at the ready to drain the item you are frying.

Recipe Measurements

I've written the recipes in traditional imperial measurements: teaspoons, tablespoons, cups, and so on. The one thing I will add is: Don't get too hung up on the measurements being exact. If you go to the store and buy one cucumber and it ends up being a little less than what we called for, don't bother making a second trip to the store. If you're baking, you need to follow recipes precisely, but when you're cooking you have a lot more leeway.

How to Buy Seafood

Before I get into the nuts and bolts of shopping for ingredients, I want to try to take some of the stress out of buying seafood. Seafood is amazing in the sense that it is one of the few wild species of protein that you can buy in a store. But we hear so many buzzwords associated with seafood: sustainable, wild-caught, farmed, local, organic, previously frozen, all natural, and so on. You can choose to read into them, or you can take them for what they are—marketing terms meant to make the buyer feel like they're making the right choice.

A basic starting point should be this: You are not doing anything wrong by selecting any of these choices. It's true that some seafood is a better choice than others for a variety of reasons. But if you're standing at a fish counter, you can feel good about almost any choice you make. Seafood is, for the most part, a healthy protein.

Educate yourself about what is good, but don't ever feel intimidated. Remember: All seafood choices are good choices.

A few things I always keep in mind:

• There are many excellent choices in farmed seafood. And, it's the way of the future. I believe that responsible fish farming is going to become essential to how we feed our planet in years to come.

• Sustainable can mean many things, such as maintaining stock limits or using minimally invasive catch methods—don't let the term take on too much weight.

• Buy local. When you support a local fishing fleet, you are supporting an industry. I feel that fishermen and women are sometimes made out to be villains who are trying to empty the ocean.

That is not the case. Fishermen and women are stewards of the waterways who understand that these resources need to be looked after if we want to have seafood available to us in the future. Plus, the less distance your seafood has to travel, the better.

• Eat a variety of seafoods. Salmon and shrimp are great standbys, but there are so many amazing species that should be a part of your regular meal plan.

Basic Tips for Buying, Handling, and Storing Seafood

Buy fish from a store or counter that is busy. Generally, the quicker a store turns over inventory, the better.

Fresh fish and seafood should not have an odor. Far away or up close, fish should smell somewhat neutral or slightly sweet.

Buy whole fish if you can. The only way truly to judge seafood is to see the complete fish. It should be bright in appearance with clear eyes, scales intact, and bright red gills. It should be firm to the touch and have an overall healthy appearance. A good fish counter will be able to clean it for you by removing the scales and guts.

If you can't buy a whole fish, look for filets with a bright, clean appearance. They should not be sitting in liquid and the flesh should feel tacky, not slimy.

Lobsters should only be bought when they're alive. I don't like buying cooked lobsters—you want to know the condition of the lobster before it was cooked. It's better to cook them at home. Buying freshly shucked lobster meat is also an option, albeit an expensive one, that involves way less work.

If you're buying shellfish, ask to see the shellfish tag. All live shellfish should have a tag listing where it was harvested and when. Oysters, clams, and mussels all have these tags. If the harvest date was more than six or seven days prior, look for something else.

Scallops should be ivory white and tacky. You want dry scallops; sometimes scallops are soaked in a solution that causes water absorption and increases shelf life. If they're sitting in liquid, pass on them. Scallops in the shell should still be alive.

All seafood is on a timer as soon as it leaves the water. Cook fish no more than two days after you purchase it, and if possible I suggest cooking it within twenty-four hours of bringing it home.

Fish and shellfish should never sit in standing water. If you are setting fresh seafood over ice, make sure that when the ice melts it will not be sitting in water.

Frozen and previously frozen seafood are still good options. Well-handled frozen fish can be great, especially since some seafood has to travel a long way. Take your time thawing it out: overnight in the refrigerator is best. Some fish may be labeled PF, or previously frozen. Sometimes a store buys frozen fish and thaws it out a little at a time as it sells it. No matter whether it has been frozen or not, it should meet all of the criteria previously mentioned, including those for odor and appearance.

Lastly, always go in with a backup plan and remain flexible. Many recipes can work with several species of fish or shellfish. Be ready to look for alternatives. You might find a new favorite. And, if you become a regular at a fish counter, the team behind it will be happy to coach you on new ideas and options.

The Oyster Primer

When we first opened Row 34 in 2013, a conversation around oysters usually started with us describing where the oysters were from, maybe a bit about who grew them, and an introduction to the term merroir, which refers to the way the environment—location, water temperature, algae, and even wind direction—contributes to the flavor of an oyster.

Today, our conversations go far deeper than just how an oyster tastes. We're talking more and more about what oyster farming means on many other levels. Most oysters you find on restaurant menus these days are farmed, not wild. We've depleted most of our wild stocks to the point that many are now in protected areas and can't be harvested for commercial use. So, farmers in coastal communities around the country are using practical, noninvasive equipment to grow oysters from seed. When people hear the phrase "farmed seafood," they sometimes react negatively, as they may have learned negative things about some types of seafood farming. But rest assured that oyster farming is a type of aquaculture you can feel good about.

Oyster farmers are, deep down, environmentalists and coastal stewards. By growing oysters in a specific bay or harbor, they're adding to that waterway's ecosystem. Oysters are filter feeders, so they essentially clean the water around them, which can quickly have a positive impact on the ecosystem. They help create algae and phytoplankton, which draws fish and bolsters the life of a waterway. Plus, oystermen and women are often strongly rooted in their local communities—and in many cases those communities have been hit hard by the diminishing fishing and lobstering industries. By bringing oyster farming into small coastal towns, these stewards are not only feeding their own families—they're also putting money and opportunity back into those communities.

As you set out on your own oyster journey, consider that each oyster is doing far more than resting on a beautiful platter and providing a taste of the ocean. Oysters are part of a much larger system that is helping our environment and reviving our coastal communities.

Oyster Basics

There are five species of oysters that grow in the United States. Within those species there are thousands of varieties, but in general knowing the species of the oyster you're eating will help you understand what you're about to taste.

EASTERN (*CRASSOSTREA VIRGINICA*)

These oysters are native to the United States. They grow up and down the eastern seaboard from Nova Scotia to Texas. They exude merroir, meaning they take on the flavors of their environment more than any other species. And they're tough, both in surviving the elements and in texture—they've usually got a good chew to them. These can be large or small and range from mild to super briny.

PACIFIC (*CRASSOSTREA GIGAS*)

These oysters were brought over from the Miyagi Prefecture of northern Japan in the 1950s and were planted on the West Coast. They are a fast-growing oyster and they're the most commonly grown oyster in the world. These can be large or small and are a bit sweet with notes of cucumber.

KUMAMOTO (*CRASSOSTREA SIKAMEA*)

Originally, these oysters came from the Nagasaki area of Japan and are now grown in the Pacific Northwest. These are considered a good starter oyster since they're firm and sometimes sweet with lots of melon and honeydew flavors.

EUROPEAN FLAT OR BELON (*OSTREA EDULIS*)

These European oysters were brought over to the coast of Maine by researchers in the 1950s. They now grow wild along parts of the northeastern coast of the United States and even down into Massachusetts. The shells are very flat and round. The flavor is challenging; they're quite metallic, almost coppery tasting, with a sharp finish.

OLYMPIA (*OSTREA CONCHAPHILA*)

These are the only native species of North America besides *Virginica* (Eastern) oysters. Tiny in size, they are big in flavor. They're very slow-growing oysters that can be fragile and temperamental. Unfortu-

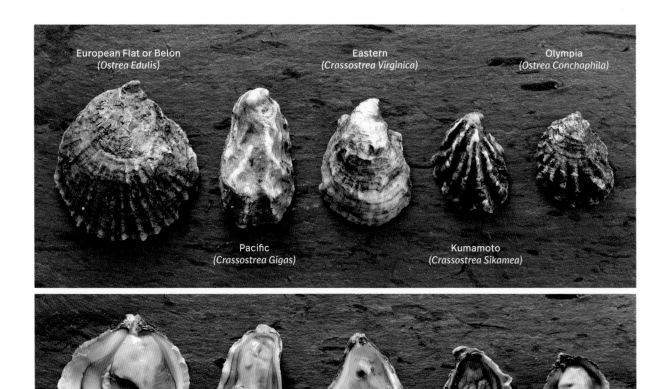

European Flat or Belon
(Ostrea Edulis)

Eastern
(Crassostrea Virginica)

Olympia
(Ostrea Conchaphila)

Pacific
(Crassostrea Gigas)

Kumamoto
(Crassostrea Sikamea)

nately, wild stocks have been depleted, but some farmers are having success growing them in the Pacific Northwest. The primary flavor is copper, but these can be rich and briny as well.

I recommend *A Geography of Oysters: The Connoisseur's Guide to Oyster Eating in North America* by Rowan Jacobsen (Bloomsbury, 2007) if you are looking for a more comprehensive reference guide.

Oyster Geography

Northeast: From Nova Scotia to the mid-Atlantic, you'll find oysters with big brine that provide lots of opportunity to taste a range of merroir that varies from state to state and even from cove to cove. Several established oyster companies thrive, but more and more small growers are coming online each year.

South: From the mid-Atlantic down through Texas, oysters can vary drastically. The brine might not be as prevalent in Southern oysters, but there's plenty of variety. The South is also the fastest-growing oyster farming region in America—in just a few years thirteen new oyster

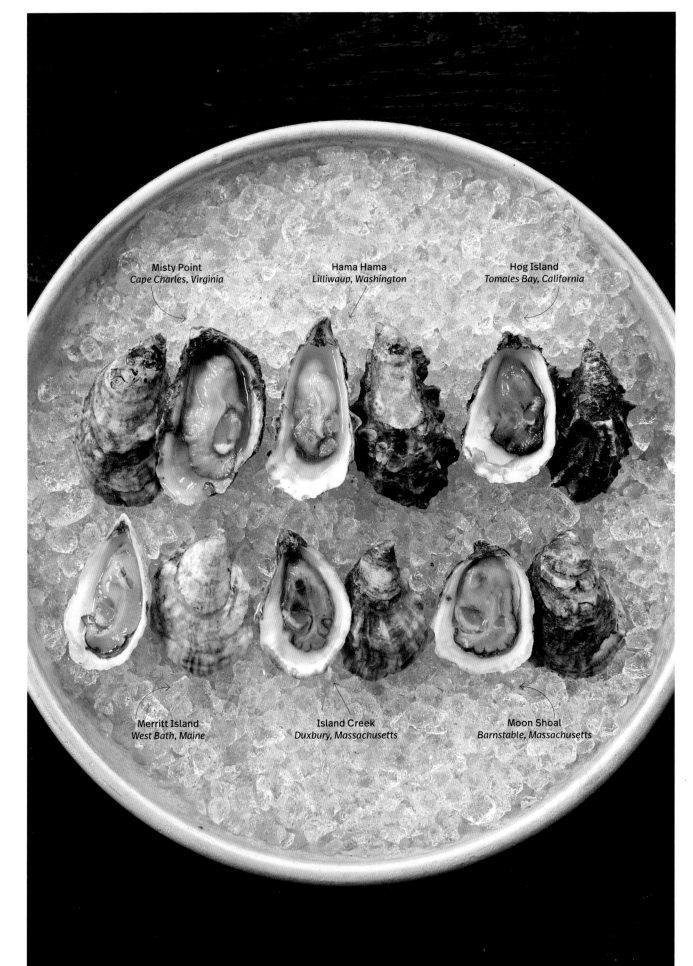

Misty Point
Cape Charles, Virginia

Hama Hama
Lilliwaup, Washington

Hog Island
Tomales Bay, California

Merritt Island
West Bath, Maine

Island Creek
Duxbury, Massachusetts

Moon Shoal
Barnstable, Massachusetts

farms opened in Alabama alone, and there are now farms operating in every Southern coastal state.

West: Here you'll find several species, including Pacifics, Kumamotos, and Olympias. Flavor profiles vary up and down the West Coast, but often, you'll get bright flavors like melon and cucumber, as well as minimal brine.

Six Oyster Growers to Know

It's hard for me to pick a favorite oyster farm, or even narrow it down to six. But I've chosen to highlight these because they mean something to me personally or they are strong growing operations in their regions.

Hama Hama Oysters | Lilliwaup, Washington | Grower: Adam James
The Pacific Northwest is stunningly beautiful—a raw, rugged area that has a unique feel to it. It's easy to get lost there, and yet it definitely has a sense of place. The James family has been growing oysters and logging in this area for decades. I've eaten Hama Hama oysters many times and they are a perfect example of what a great oyster from the area should be: a plump deep oyster with firm texture and a great vegetal flavor.

Hog Island Oyster Co. | Tomales Bay, California | Grower: John Finger
My love for oysters started in Tomales Bay at Hog Island. I was a chef in Northern California, and the staff took a trip to the farm. Back then, it was a humble version of what it has grown into—but my education started right there. I had enjoyed oysters plenty of times before, but eating them straight from the water turned something on for me. Hog Island has its own incredible oyster bars in California; that's where most of the farm's oysters go. But occasionally I get to serve them in New England. The flavor always brings me back to Tomales Bay: sweet minerality makes these a West Coast standout.

Island Creek Oysters | Duxbury, Massachusetts | Grower: Skip Bennett
One of my greatest and most accidental accomplishments is that I was the first chef ever to visit the Island Creek Oysters farm in Duxbury. A few staff members and I drove down to meet Skip and see what he was growing. It was a small operation then run by Skip and a few of his buddies—now it's grown into something outstanding. Skip put Duxbury on the oyster map in his own rogue way, typical of an oyster farmer. During that visit, I found my East Coast version of Hog Island oysters and for years they were the only oysters I served. The original Island Creek is still one of the best oysters ever, and now Skip's farm is growing several different varieties. He has taught me more about

oysters than anyone—and I still love eating his. The briny pop makes them a delicious example of an East Coast oyster.

Moon Shoal Oysters | Barnstable, Massachusetts | Grower: Jon Martin
The conditions in Barnstable are just right for growing amazing oysters, and Moon Shoal Oysters is in one of the best spots on Cape Cod, in my opinion. Although it's hard to pick one farm to highlight from this area, Moon Shoal oysters have always stood out to me. Jon was once a firefighter and switched gears to grow oysters—and he always seems to be having a great time doing it. His oysters grow in open trays on the sandy bay floor. Their salty and buttery flavor is hard not to love.

Merritt Island Oysters | West Bath, Maine | Grower: Jordi St. John
With its many islands, Maine has more coastline than any other state. In recent years Maine has also added more oyster farmers than any other state—making it hard to nail down just one favorite. But if I had to, it would be Merritt Island. With massive tides and cold, algae-rich water, the New Meadows River helps provide a flavor that balances between vegetal and briny. Small to medium in size with a deep cup, Merritt Island oysters are a great example of what a Maine oyster can be.

Cherrystone Aqua-Farms | Cape Charles, Virginia | Grower: Tim Rapine
A lot of oysters are grown on Virginia's eastern shore, and many of them are really good. I love the Misty Point oysters from Cherrystone Aqua-Farms because they have a little more flavor complexity than the other oysters available in the area. They are grown in floating cages and get knocked around on both tides, which gives them a nice cup. The flavor is salt up-front, which gives way to seaweed and mossy tones on the finish.

How to Order Oysters

EATING OUT

If you're new to ordering oysters in a restaurant, don't be intimidated. It's okay if you don't know what to do. I like to eat oysters in a place that sells different varieties, so I recommend finding a place with a good oyster list. The best way to start is by asking what's most popular and begin with those. Anyone selling oysters should be willing and able to help coach you through the process. Ask a lot of questions, like where the oysters are from and how they're grown. At a good oyster spot, they'll know. I also recommend starting small: Pick two or three varieties to taste together. Try them with a squeeze of lemon or a little

CONTINUED ON PAGE 27 →

How to Shuck Oysters

Like any task in the kitchen, shucking oysters takes practice. It's an empowering feeling, though, to shuck an oyster properly—and a great party trick.

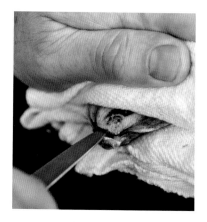
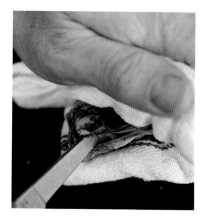
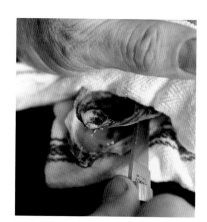

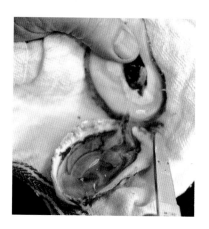
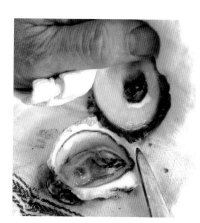
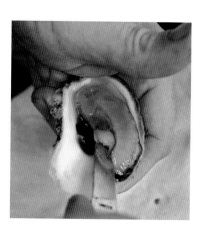

Step 1. Wash your oysters thoroughly under cold running water, scrubbing the outside of the shells. Do not let them sit in the water; move them to a cutting board. Prepare a platter by lining it with a few paper towels and then covering the platter with crushed ice. Prepare your sauces (page 33), lemon wedges (page 43), and crackers (page 221).

Step 2. Place an oyster cup-side down on a towel. Fold the towel partway over the top of the oyster, making sure the hinge is exposed. This will protect your non-shucking hand.

Step 3. Hold the oyster down firmly against the surface with the palm of your non-shucking hand. The towel should create a barrier between your hand and the oyster.

Step 4. Place the tip of a shucking knife inside the hinge between the top and bottom shells. Push the tip into the hinge; twist the knife back and forth until you feel the hinge pop.

Step 5. Open the top shell of the oyster just enough to slide the oyster knife along the inside of the top shell to loosen the meat from the shell.

Step 6. Holding the oyster level so the liquor does not run out, carefully loosen the bottom muscle from its shell, so the oyster is "floating" in the cup of the bottom shell.

What to Pair with Oysters

by Suzanne Hays, General Manager / Beer Director, Row 34

When people think of oyster pairings, Champagne typically comes to mind. Before this elegant duo came to be the default, however, bivalves had a more humble companion: beer. Porters would sit by the docks crushing oysters and pints before heading back to work. Oysters were once a working-class food, and beer was their drink. Beer is the pairing that I prefer for oysters, and one we encourage at Row 34.

When considering a solid pairing, think about the characteristics of the oyster itself and try to complement the flavors without overpowering them. No matter what you choose, whether you're a hophead or prefer Champagne, pairing beverages and oysters should be fun.

These are a few of our go-to recommendations.

New England IPAs: These juicy brews provide a good balance to the brine of most eastern (*Virginica*) oysters.

Sour Beers: Sip on these with a super-briny Wellfleet. The beer's tart citrus will balance out the oyster's salinity, acting in place of a lemon wedge.

Porters and Stouts: These make a surprisingly great match to most briny oysters. Their roasty, dry characteristics bring out an oyster's brightness.

Goses: A Gose's mild salinity and coriander complement the sweetness of Kumamotos, which are delicate and known for their fruity, melon-like flavors.

Saisons: Saisons are effervescent and bready, with the incredible ability to pair well with just about anything. If you're a bold hero who enjoys the copperlike intensity of a Belon, pair it with a saison, which can stand up to strong flavors.

mignonette to get started. Or, if you want the full experience, just eat them with nothing on top—you'll be surprised at the different flavor profiles you detect.

For the more advanced oyster lover, I suggest going deeper into both geography and species. Eating a West Coast oyster next to an East Coast oyster is a great way to taste the difference. The primary species grown on the West Coast is Pacific, or Gigas, which is grown from Canada all the way down the California coast. On the East Coast and along the Gulf, the species of oyster is Eastern, or Virginica. Try eating those two species next to one another and you'll quickly understand how they differ. Remember that how and where an oyster is grown absolutely influences how it tastes. Eating an oyster from Duxbury next to an oyster from Chatham or Charleston (all Virginicas) will show you just how much variation you can find in each species. The white whale in oyster tasting is getting all five species on the same tray. Kumamoto, Olympia, and Gigas from the West Coast and Virginica and Belon from the East Coast. It's the ultimate oyster experience.

Oysters should always be served on a tray of ice so that they sit flat and the oyster liquor remains in the shell. The meat should look like someone lifted the top shell off with no effort. The meat should be plump and in one piece, barely disturbed. I like mine with lemon and sometimes classic mignonette—but eat them however you like.

I always suggest starting small and eating local. I'm a firm believer that oysters eaten near the water somehow taste better. Great oysters are available all year long, but I enjoy getting East Coast oysters during the spring and summer and tend to eat more West Coast oysters in the colder months. New varieties of oysters are always popping up, and tasting an oyster for the first time still brings me great joy—I hope it does the same for you.

EATING AT HOME

Opening oysters at home is a basic kitchen skill. Oysters are meant to be communal, so tasting oysters is a great excuse to invite friends over to share in the fun. Your first stop should be a good local fish market to see what kind of variety they have. If you don't have a good market nearby, or the variety isn't great, go directly to an oyster farm and have oysters delivered. You'll probably find less variety when purchasing from a single source, but buying from a farm that grows and ships directly is the best option for getting fresh, just-out-of-the-water oysters. (There are several e-commerce sites that sell seafood, which can also be good options.) However you order them, the oysters should be shipped directly overnight and come with information on both the harvest date and the grower. I like to connect the dots back to the water; finding out where they're grown helps me feel more connected. The oysters should arrive cold, with no odor, and they should be surrounded by ice packs that are still a little frozen.

Oyster Bars: A Very Brief History

The history of oyster bars or, as they were once called, oyster saloons, gives us a peek into the history of this country. Traditionally, oyster saloons were neighborhood spots in urban centers that served freshly shucked oysters and cold beer. In the mid-1800s there were actually thousands of oyster bars spread throughout the major U.S. cites. The railroad brought oysters to the middle of the country, and after the Gold Rush in California, people stayed on the West Coast and enjoyed oysters out there. Pushcarts, saloons, and high-end oyster eateries were scattered all across America.

Oysters were a fairly common food back in the late eighteenth and nineteenth centuries. They were readily available and cheap, which led to the birth of the oyster bar. When oysters are left alone to grow in the wild, they create massive living reefs. Back then, these oyster reefs were thriving and could feed entire communities. Oyster beds could be found up and down the East Coast, with the biggest supply coming from New York, Boston Harbor, and especially Chesapeake Bay.

As with so many things that humans love, we eventually indulged too much. We overharvested the oyster beds, and soon the Industrial Revolution caused pollution that severely damaged many coastal oyster habitats. The neighborhood oyster bar started to disappear. Oysters never went away, of course. They were still available but became a luxury. Eventually, though, oyster farming, which has been done in this country since the eighteenth century, became modernized, which is why we've seen a resurgence in the American oyster. Today, these bivalves are a staple on menus of establishments ranging from casual pubs to the finest high-end restaurants in the world. The effort that goes into growing oysters has now earned the respect of chefs everywhere. With the return of the oyster, we are witnessing a return of the neighborhood oyster bar.

Even more significantly, we're now seeing many efforts to restore oyster habitats. The Billion Oyster Project, founded in 2014, is replanting and restoring oyster reefs around New York Harbor by working with students and volunteers. The University of New Hampshire has part-

nered with the Nature Conservancy to help restore oyster populations in the Great Bay Estuary. And the Chesapeake Bay Foundation has enlisted hundreds of volunteers to produce oyster gardens along their own pieces of shoreline.

Today, the American oyster bar is returning to neighborhoods and communities around the country. There are many things that make up a great oyster bar, and everyone has their own opinion on what those are. For me, it's a warm, inviting atmosphere where the oysters are on full display. The energy of an oyster bar is unique—something you don't find in other restaurants. A good oyster bar should give a nod of love to local oysters. And the menu should offer a taste of the region. In New England, that might be fried clams or lobster rolls. In the South, it's hush puppies and gumbo. The West Coast will show off Dungeness crab and Manila clams. From the little jewel that is The Walrus and the Carpenter in Seattle to the sprawling Grand Central Oyster Bar in Manhattan, oyster bars are celebrating the best of these briny bivalves, and I'm happy to see so many more becoming neighborhood spots, just as they were always meant to be.

CHAPTER ONE

It All Starts with Oysters

Raw Oysters with Cocktail Sauce, Classic Mignonette, and Spicy Mignonette

These are the sauces that we serve with most raw bar items. The sauces can be made a few days in advance and refrigerated. I don't personally love cocktail sauce on oysters, but a little freshly grated horseradish on an oyster might change your life. If you can't find fresh horseradish, simply use all prepared (jarred) horseradish in the cocktail sauce. And if you like some heat, use a jalapeño instead of a Fresno pepper in the spicy mignonette.

Place a few paper towels on the bottom of a large, rimmed tray (stainless steel works well) and fill with crushed ice or small ice pellets.

Pour each sauce into individual ramekins and place the ramekins in the center of the oyster platter.

Using the instructions on page 25, shuck the oysters, making sure to cut the meat completely from the shell; discard the tops and arrange the oysters on top of the crushed ice. Scatter lemon wedges around the ice and serve immediately.

Cocktail Sauce

If using fresh horseradish, peel it and use a microplane to grate it into a medium bowl. You should have about 2 tablespoons. Add the remaining ingredients to the bowl and stir until combined.

MAKES 24 OYSTERS, 4 TO 6 SERVINGS

¼ cup Cocktail Sauce (below)

¼ cup Classic Mignonette (following page)

¼ cup Spicy Mignonette (following page)

24 medium oysters

8 lemon wedges (see page 43)

FOR THE COCKTAIL SAUCE

MAKES ABOUT 2 CUPS

One 2-inch piece fresh horseradish

3 tablespoons prepared horseradish

1 cup ketchup

1 cup chili sauce

1 tablespoon Tabasco sauce

1 tablespoon Worcestershire sauce

2 tablespoons freshly squeezed lemon juice

2 teaspoons kosher salt

1 teaspoon freshly ground black pepper

FOR THE CLASSIC MIGNONETTE

MAKES ABOUT 1 CUP

1 large shallot, minced

½ cup dry white wine

½ cup champagne vinegar

1 teaspoon freshly ground black pepper

FOR THE SPICY MIGNONETTE

MAKES ABOUT 1 CUP

½ cup dry white wine

½ cup champagne vinegar

1 Fresno pepper, stem, ribs, and seeds removed

1 teaspoon sriracha hot sauce

1 large shallot, minced

2 tablespoons chopped cilantro

1 teaspoon freshly ground black pepper

Classic Mignonette

In a medium bowl, combine the shallot, wine, and vinegar. Season with the black pepper just before serving.

Spicy Mignonette

Place the wine, vinegar, Fresno pepper, and sriracha in a blender and puree until smooth. Strain through a sieve into a medium bowl and stir in the shallot. Just before serving add the chopped cilantro and season with black pepper.

Fried Oysters with Lemon and Tartar Sauce

You want to use plump, larger oysters for frying. Make sure the meat is whole and in good condition. Fried oysters are great with almost any sauce, but tartar sauce is a classic choice. Make sure to eat these while they're still warm. If you're making a half portion (for the Oyster Burgers with Togarashi Aïoli on page 129, for example), simply cut the ingredient list in half. And before you start, be sure to refer to Frying Seafood at Home on page 15.

In a large bowl, combine the oysters with the buttermilk and Tabasco sauce. Refrigerate for 30 minutes.

Line a large plate with paper towels and set aside. In a heavy, straight-sided skillet or Dutch oven, heat the canola oil to 350° F.

Meanwhile, pour the flour into a shallow bowl. Drain the liquid off the oysters and toss each oyster in the flour. The oysters should be well coated.

Shake off excess flour and carefully place the oysters in the frying oil; do this in batches if necessary. Fry the oysters until very crisp but not overcooked, about 2 minutes. The oysters should be crisp on the outside, creamy in the middle, and warm all the way through.

Using a slotted spoon or skimmer, remove the oysters from the oil and drain on the prepared plate. Immediately season the oysters with salt and pepper. To serve, spread the tartar sauce on small serving plates and place a few fried oysters on top of the sauce. Garnish with lemon wedges and parsley leaves. Or, double the amount of parsley leaves and scatter the leaves onto a platter, then place the oysters on top and serve with the sauce and lemon wedges on the side.

MAKES 24 OYSTERS, 4 TO 6 SERVINGS

24 medium to large oysters, shucked

½ cup buttermilk

1 tablespoon Tabasco sauce

4 cups canola oil for frying

2 cups Seasoned Flour (page 229)

Kosher salt and freshly ground black pepper

½ cup Tartar Sauce (page 224)

4 to 6 lemon wedges (see page 43)

12 flat-leaf parsley leaves

Lettuce Cups with Crispy Oysters and Pickled Vegetables

MAKES 12 CUPS, 4 TO 6 SERVINGS

2 cups canola oil

1 cup rice flour

12 large oysters, shucked

Kosher salt to taste

12 large leaves Bibb lettuce

½ cup Togarashi Aïoli (page 225)

½ cup Pickled Vegetables
(page 214)

This is a simple and fun oyster dish that's great to share with a group—and it's gluten free. To add some color to the pickles, incorporate ¼ cup thinly shaved red cabbage. One good head of Bibb lettuce should provide the dozen leaves needed for this recipe; it's best to use the larger outer leaves.

Line a large plate with paper towels and set aside. In a heavy, straight-sided skillet or Dutch oven, heat the canola oil to 350° F.

Meanwhile, place the rice flour in a shallow bowl. Drain any liquid off the oysters and toss them with the rice flour until they are well coated. Shake off excess flour, then carefully place the oysters in the hot oil; do this in batches if necessary. Fry until the oysters are light brown and crispy, about 90 seconds. The oysters should be crisp on the outside, creamy in the middle, and warm all the way through. Use a slotted spoon or skimmer to remove the oysters and transfer to the prepared plate. Season with salt.

To serve, arrange the Bibb lettuce leaves in a single layer on a platter and place a small dollop of aïoli in the center of each leaf. Place some of the pickled vegetables over the aïoli and top each portion with a fried oyster. Finish with another dollop of aïoli on top of each oyster and serve.

Grilled Oysters with Lemon-Garlic Butter

This is the perfect summertime outdoor recipe that is both easy and delicious. These are great eaten right out of the shell—with or without the toast. This recipe also works with clams. Don't overcook the oysters. Let them warm through on the outside edges of a grill. When the butter is bubbling, it's time to eat.

Heat a grill to medium heat.

Place the sourdough slices on the grill and toast lightly, 1 to 2 minutes per side. Cut each into 3 evenly sized pieces and set aside.

Shuck the oysters, leaving the meat in the shells. Divide the butter among the oysters, giving about 1 generous teaspoon to each, and carefully place them on the grill. (Melting butter will flare up if it drips, so try to place them around the edge if the flame is high.) Watch for the butter to bubble and then grill until the oysters are firm to the touch, about 1 minute after the butter starts to bubble.

Sprinkle the oysters with parsley and a pinch of salt. Serve with the grilled sourdough bread.

MAKES 18 OYSTERS, 4 TO 6 SERVINGS

6 large slices sourdough bread

18 medium to large oysters

4 ounces Lemon-Garlic Butter (page 226), at room temperature

2 tablespoons flat-leaf parsley leaves, cut into strips

Sea salt

Baked Oysters with Smoked Uni Butter and Parsley Crumbs

18 medium oysters

½ cup kosher salt, plus more for seasoning

½ cup white breadcrumbs

¼ cup flat-leaf parsley leaves

1 teaspoon finely grated lemon zest

1 teaspoon red pepper flakes

2 ounces Smoked Uni Butter (page 227)

1 large shallot, minced

Freshly ground black pepper

Smoked uni butter and oysters are both naturally a little salty—in this dish be careful when adding any extra seasoning. The oysters can be assembled a day ahead and kept cold until ready to bake. Let them sit at room temperature for about 20 minutes before baking. The red pepper flakes add a little bit of heat but can easily be omitted. For a variation, remove the oysters from their shells and place them in a small, buttered baking dish; bake with the melted butter and breadcrumbs scattered over the top.

Preheat the oven to 450° F. Shuck the oysters and place the oyster meat in a bowl. Refrigerate until ready to assemble. Clean out and reserve the bottom shells; discard the top shells.

In a small bowl, mix the salt with a little water to make a thick paste that sticks together. Place 18 teaspoon-sized mounds of the salt paste on a baking sheet—these will hold the oysters upright and level. Place an oyster shell on each pile of salt paste and place one piece of oyster meat back in each shell.

In a food processor, pulse together the breadcrumbs, parsley, lemon zest, and red pepper flakes until the parsley is thoroughly incorporated with the breadcrumbs; they should take on a green color.

In a small saucepan, melt the uni butter over low heat. Stir in the shallot, season lightly with salt and pepper, and cook until the shallot is just softened, 2 to 3 minutes. Spoon a little of the butter mixture over each oyster, then top generously with the parsley breadcrumbs. Bake until the breadcrumbs are lightly toasted and the oysters are warmed through, 8 to 10 minutes.

Serve right on the baking sheet or transfer the shells to a serving platter and fix them in place with more mounds of salt paste.

How to Clean and Store Shellfish

The most important thing to remember is that shellfish are alive. Shellfish should be in good shape, with no cracks or chips in the shells, and they should be sealed tightly. If they are open, they should quickly close with a gentle tap.

How to Store Them

Never cover shellfish in plastic or store them in a sealed container. If you are putting shellfish on ice, make sure that when the ice melts the water can easily drain so that the shellfish are not sitting in fresh water, which will kill them. And don't soak your shellfish to clean them or soak them in water to purge any sand—again, sitting in fresh water will kill them. Always keep your shellfish cold and use within a day or two of buying. To store them in your fridge, leave them in the netting they came in (if they came in a container wrapped in plastic, remove the plastic completely). Place them either in a bowl or on a baking sheet. Leave uncovered or place a damp cloth on top of them.

To Clean Mussels:

Place the mussels in a colander and run cold water over them to remove any external dirt or sand. Most mussels have a little piece on the side called the beard that is easily removed by pulling on it. Cleaning and removing the beard should be done just before cooking.

To Clean Clams and Oysters:

Place the clams or oysters in a colander and run cold water over them. Using a dedicated brush, scrub each shell under the water to remove any external dirt and sand.

How to Build a Raw Bar Platter

Eating shellfish is a communal and festive experience, and a simple raw bar platter should be eaten with friends whenever possible. Below are a few guidelines, but you can really make a platter your own by adding or subtracting whatever you'd like. Don't forget to include chips in a separate bowl on the same table for the ceviche. (See page 216 to make your own chips.)

What You Need

Large rimmed platter (stainless steel works best)

Paper towels

Crushed ice or small ice pellets

2 small ramekins

2 small bowls

Shellfish forks for serving

Line the bottom of a rimmed platter with a couple of paper towels. Top with a level layer of crushed ice or ice pellets.

Fill two small ramekins, one with mignonette and one with cocktail sauce, and place in the center of the ice.

Next, put the lemon wedges at either end of the platter. Place the shucked oysters together along the left edge of the platter.

Place the shucked littlenecks in rows beside the oysters. Place the cooked shrimp in a pile at one end of the platter.

Place the two types of ceviche in two small bowls and place them at either end of the platter atop the ice. Offer shellfish forks on the side. Serve immediately.

SERVES 4

¼ cup Classic Mignonette (page 34)

¼ cup Cocktail Sauce (page 33)

6 lemon wedges (see below)

12 medium oysters, shucked (see instructions on page 25)

8 littleneck clams, shucked (see instructions on page 114)

12 cooked shrimp (see Shrimp Cocktail recipe, page 103)

1 batch Striped Bass Ceviche with Grilled Corn and Fresno Pepper (page 95)

1 batch Scallop Ceviche with Cilantro Pesto (page 92)

How to Cut a Lemon Wedge

Rinse a medium lemon under water, then dry. Trim each pointy end off. Cut the lemon equally in half from end to end. Cut the half in half lengthwise and then do that again, so you end up with 8 equally sized wedges. Lay each wedge on its side and trim the thin white strip away from the center of each wedge. Use the tip of a paring knife to carefully flick out any exposed seeds. If not using the lemon wedges right away, keep them wrapped in plastic so they do not dry out.

Poached Oysters with Hollandaise and Caviar

Don't toss those oyster shells. Anytime you're shucking oysters, save the pretty, well-shaped, deep-cup shells and clean them out so you can use them for times like this—they'll last for years. For this recipe, look for medium-sized oysters with a deep cup. You'll want to finish this just before serving, and if you have a minute, warm up the oyster shells in the oven right before you assemble them. Serve these as soon as they're assembled—it's one of my favorite ways to enjoy cooked oysters.

Mix the salt with 3 tablespoons water to make a paste, then use the paste to make 18 small mounds on a platter; these will hold the clean oyster shells and keep them upright.

Shuck the oysters, saving the meat and any oyster liquor in a bowl. Discard the top shells and clean out the bottom shells and place on top of the salt mounds on the platter.

Combine the stock, Pernod, and bay leaf in a medium saucepan and bring to a boil. Add the oysters and any reserved liquor to the saucepan and return to a simmer. Remove the pan from the heat and let the oysters poach in the warm liquid for 5 minutes. Using a slotted spoon, remove the oysters from the liquid, placing each one in a clean oyster shell. Coat each oyster generously with warm hollandaise and top each with the caviar. Serve immediately.

MAKES 18 OYSTERS, 4 TO 6 SERVINGS

1 cup kosher salt

18 medium oysters

1½ cups Vegetable Stock (page 230)

¼ cup Pernod

1 bay leaf

1 cup Hollandaise Sauce (following page)

1 ounce caviar, preferably white sturgeon or osetra

MAKES ABOUT 1 CUP

2 sticks (16 tablespoons) unsalted
   butter

¼ cup apple cider vinegar

2 sprigs thyme

2 whole peppercorns

1 bay leaf

2 large egg yolks

¼ teaspoon Tabasco sauce

½ teaspoon freshly squeezed
   lemon juice

Kosher salt and freshly ground
   black pepper

Hollandaise Sauce

Melt the butter in a small saucepan over low heat. If it begins to foam, skim the foam. Once the butter is melted, keep warm. In another small saucepan, combine the cider vinegar, thyme, peppercorns, and bay leaf and set over medium-high heat; simmer to reduce until only about 1 tablespoon of liquid remains. Set aside to cool slightly.

In a stainless steel mixing bowl, whisk together the egg yolks and 1 tablespoon water. Strain the vinegar reduction into the mixture, discarding the solids. In a saucepan that is large enough that the stainless steel bowl will rest on top, bring a few inches of water to a simmer. Place the bowl with the egg mixture on top of the saucepan and whisk until the yolk mixture doubles in volume and thickens.

Remove the saucepan, with the bowl still on top, from the heat. Slowly whisk the melted butter into the yolk mixture until it emulsifies. Add a few drops of cool water if the sauce becomes too thick. Stir in the Tabasco sauce and lemon juice. Season with salt and pepper and keep warm.

Smoked Oysters in Olive Oil

Smoked oysters remind me of my dad. I remember sitting with him while he ate them out of a can, sticking each one with a toothpick before devouring it. I eventually worked up the courage to try one—it was the first piece of smoked seafood I ever tasted, and I still love them to this day. Now, I make them for myself with this easy method. Look for full-size oysters, which will result in large, meaty pieces.

In a medium saucepan, bring the brine to a simmer over medium-high heat. Add the oysters, then lower the heat to a gentle simmer and let it just bubble for 1 to 2 minutes, no more. Remove the pan from the heat. Let the oysters and brine cool down to room temperature. Drain the oysters.

Preheat the oven (preferably a convection oven with a fan) to 250°F.

Pat the oysters dry with paper towels and place on a perforated tray or rack inside a smoking container with a tight-fitting lid or plastic wrap. Use a smoking gun to apply smoke to the container, cover, and let the oysters sit for 15 minutes. (See instructions on page 55.) Turn the oysters over and smoke for another 10 minutes. Add smoke 3 to 4 times during the process. Remove the oysters and place in the oven for 12 more minutes. The oysters should be cooked through and have a firm texture. Once the oysters are firm, refrigerate until chilled, then place them in a jar with a tight-fitting lid. Fill the jar with the olive oil, which should cover all of the oysters completely. Refrigerate until ready to serve. Drain the oysters and place them on a platter for serving, or eat them straight out of the jar using toothpicks. Stored in the refrigerator, they will keep for up to 7 days.

MAKES 24 OYSTERS, 4 TO 6 SERVINGS

3 cups Basic Brine (page 56)

24 large oysters, shucked

1 cup extra-virgin olive oil

Angels on Horseback

MAKES 18 OYSTERS, 4 TO 6
SERVINGS

9 slices bacon

18 medium to large oysters,
    shucked

4 lemon wedges (see page 43)

¼ cup Grain Mustard Aïoli
    (page 225)

This is a tasty and easy oyster recipe that you can pull off quickly. These are meant to be finger food: Serve them with toothpicks so you can drag them through the aïoli. For this one, you can even use pre-shucked oysters if you're not up for shucking them yourself.

Preheat the oven to 350° F.

Place the bacon slices flat on a baking sheet with about ½ inch between them. Bake until slightly crispy but still pliable enough to wrap around the oysters, 15 to 18 minutes. Remove the bacon from the oven and turn up the oven to 425° F.

Let the bacon cool slightly, then cut the slices in half crosswise. Wrap each shucked oyster with a bacon slice and secure by pushing a toothpick through the oyster. Place on a clean baking sheet.

Bake the wrapped oysters until the bacon is crisp and the oysters are warmed through, about 6 minutes. Serve with lemon wedges and aïoli on the side.

Seeking Out Great Ingredients and the People Who Supply Them

After spending more than five years working in restaurants in the San Francisco Bay area, I returned to Boston to continue my cooking career on the East Coast. I loved living and working in California, because the accessibility to ingredients there was unrivaled. We had twelve months of farmer's markets, locally grown meat and poultry, and fresh seafood. It was a transformative time in my cooking life.

I have always been infatuated with ingredients and obsessed with understanding where they come from. Knowing how things are grown or how they're caught has always been important to me and constantly inspires my cooking. This may not be a unique trait in a cook, but for me, it's a North Star. It's always guiding me to new farms, new ingredients, and new kitchen techniques. Understanding how the ecosystem of food operates has helped me better appreciate all food. I love knowing about the people and processes that bring food to our plates.

While I was in California, I made my first visit to an oyster farm—it was Hog Island Oyster Co. in Tomales Bay. The farmer, John Finger, and his crew gave me an unforgettable connection to oysters. But my most life-changing oyster farm visit was to Island Creek Oysters in Duxbury, Massachusetts. I'd moved to Boston to start as the head chef of a seafood restaurant and brought a few eager chefs with me to Duxbury to visit Island Creek before we opened. The farm's humble beginnings and its farmer, Skip Bennett, spoke to me: It was a few guys doing something they loved. They were excited to share the farm with me and my crew and showed us everything we wanted to see. That day, I ate my first razor clam right out of the water, and also, my first Island Creek oyster—it was an epiphany for me as a chef. Skip and I connected over the fact that his dad, Billy, was a lobsterman, just as so many in my family in Maine have been. I'll never forget that day, getting to know Skip, his team, and his oysters.

For nearly twenty-five years, Skip has been growing Island Creek Oysters in Duxbury Bay. An oyster farm that started as an effort to recover from a failed clam business has grown into a beloved, internationally known leader in the oystering world. Skip and his crew now grow millions of oysters each year. Island Creek Oysters has a robust wholesale and retail operation, and it now has agritourism down on the farm. Meanwhile, at Island Creek they're constantly innovating their own growing processes, their hatchery, and their product. In 2010, we became partners when we opened the original Island Creek Oyster Bar in Kenmore Square.

Skip is still someone who inspires me to look at food in a particular way. Through him and other farmers, I've learned that simplicity is usually best—from the pursuit of simplicity comes great innovation, direction, and expectation. Skip's commitment to growing great oysters led him to try different methods and farming techniques, which has led him to grow other varieties of great oysters.

These days, I visit as many oyster farms as I can. I love talking to those who love what they do and are willing to share their passion with me. My interest in getting to know growing processes and the people behind the farms has continued to evolve—I seek out fishermen who act as stewards of the ocean and have respect for the wild products they catch or harvest. In addition, I look

for independent farmers who take pains to grow and sell their products at farmer's markets and to restaurants. I have gone so far as to track down a fish farm at the University of New Hampshire to learn about a certain style of aquaculture. (Read more about it on page 161.) Time spent on the water there, harvesting fish, was an education. In addition to including their fish on my menu, I wanted to be a part of that process, to see and feel every aspect of it.

This approach to food—constantly seeking to understand the people and processes behind the ingredients—has led me and my team at Row 34 to find breweries, distillers, farmers, small-batch producers, and so much more. I still get lobster from my cousin Mark, oysters from Skip, beer from my friends Dave and Dan, striper from a fisherman named Darren, and tomatoes from farmer Rick. And I'm always looking for more. Being active participants in a greater food ecosystem has become part of the DNA of Row 34—we are in constant pursuit of knowledge about what we love on the plate and in the glass.

CHAPTER TWO

Smoked and Cured, Crudo and Ceviche

Notes on Smoking Seafood

Humans have been smoking seafood in coastal communities for thousands of years. Our origins as hunters and gatherers led us to preserve what we could catch or hunt, and smoking became an excellent method of doing that. Modern smoking still provides a way to preserve meat and seafood, but now it's more about flavor than life and death.

There are many types of smoking devices out there and, therefore, many methods for smoking seafoods. For the purposes of this book—and because it's the easiest method for home cooks—I suggest investing in a smoking gun, which is a type of food smoker. The smoking gun is ideal for home cooks because it can easily smoke foods in small batches, and you can control the amount of smoke you're applying. Several manufacturers make smoking guns (I personally like the ones made by Breville), so if you find yourself enjoying the process and aim to smoke your own foods regularly, you might want to spend a little more money on a higher quality gun.

Carefully check the offerings: Some guns come with their own containers, but those may not work for all recipes. Almost all smoking guns come with wood chips that the manufacturer recommends using. For seafood, I prefer fruitwoods like apple and cherry, which provide a more subtle smoke flavor.

As you get started, remember this: The two most important parts of smoking are temperature and smoke volume. If you are using a smoking gun at home, follow the manufacturer's directions along with some of the general guidelines that I outline here. Of course, you can also use a wood or charcoal grill with a controlled fire and some wood chips—but I sometimes find that method hard to control.

When you're working with seafood, the process is equally as important as the end result. Don't be afraid to tweak your methods to get the result you're looking for.

Cold Smoking Versus Hot Smoking

Cold smoking is adding smoke flavor to something after it has been cured or brined. You are not cooking food when you cold smoke it—just adding flavor. In general, you should apply cold smoke to products that are at room temperature or below.

Hot smoking involves cooking the product as it is smoked. For the purposes of this book, I'm assuming you're hot smoking as a home cook, so the recipes call for adding smoke to the product, and then cooking it in an oven—this will give you more control over the end result.

How to Cold Smoke

Along with your smoking gun and wood chips (see previous page for preferred wood choices), you will need a large, high-sided container that is big enough to fit a perforated pan or small rack inside. The food will sit on the pan or rack so that the smoke can circulate around it on all sides. The container needs to be tightly sealed, so it should have a tight-fitting lid, or you can use plastic wrap, which works just as well. Once you've placed your item on the rack in the container, you're ready to smoke. Smoking is best done outside, as it must take place in a well-ventilated area. And make sure you read the manufacturer's instructions before you get started.

Keeping the lid or plastic wrap loosely over the container, use the smoking gun to fill the container with smoke, making sure the smoke stays inside the container. If the smoke dissipates, you can add more smoke throughout the process, being careful to keep the lid or plastic wrap over the container so the smoke doesn't escape. There should be a good amount of smoke in the container throughout the entire process.

How to Hot Smoke

For the following hot-smoked recipes, you will smoke all of the seafood using the same method described in How to Cold Smoke, with the added step of finishing every recipe by cooking the smoked item, either in an oven or on the grill. All of the hot-smoked products are cooked through; many are used in other recipes listed in this chapter.

Basic Brine

MAKES ABOUT 5 CUPS

4 cups water

1 cup kosher salt

¼ cup sugar

1 bay leaf

2 sprigs thyme

4 black peppercorns

½ teaspoon whole fennel seeds

This basic brine recipe works for many types of seafood. Always make sure that the brine is completely cool before adding the protein.

Combine all the ingredients in a stockpot and bring to a rolling boil; once the liquid is boiling, remove from the heat. Let the brine cool to room temperature, then strain out and discard all the solid ingredients.

Refrigerate until ready to use. Covered in an airtight container, the brine will keep for 2 to 3 weeks.

Basic Cure

MAKES ABOUT 5 CUPS

4 cups kosher salt

1 cup sugar

1 teaspoon whole fennel seeds

1 teaspoon ground white pepper

½ teaspoon mustard seeds

In a large bowl, stir together all ingredients, then pour them into a lidded container.

Seal the container and keep at room temperature until ready to use. Covered in an airtight container, the cure will keep for several months.

Smoked Mussels

What a great snack these are. I like to put smoked mussels into a simple pasta dish—just add some bacon and it's so good. This is another recipe that can be made a day or two in advance and added to a dish at the last minute. Look for plump mussels for this recipe; getting shells full of meat is key.

Place the mussels in a large sauté pan with a tight-fitting lid. Add the wine, stock, garlic, and shallot.

Cover the pan and bring the liquid to a simmer over medium-high heat. Steam until all of the mussels open, about 5 minutes.

Remove the pan from the heat and let cool until you're able to handle the mussels. (Remove and discard any mussels that have stubbornly refused to open.) One by one, remove the mussel meat from each shell, reserving the meat and discarding the shells. Strain the cooking liquid (line the strainer with a coffee filter or cheesecloth if you're not confident the mussels were completely purged) into a medium bowl and reserve; season the liquid with salt and pepper after straining.

Place the mussel meat on a perforated tray or rack inside a smoking container with a tight-fitting lid or plastic wrap. Use a smoking gun to apply smoke to the container, cover tightly, and let sit for 15 minutes. (See instructions on page 55.) You may want to add a little more smoke halfway through the process.

Once the mussels are smoked, return them to the reserved liquid and refrigerate until ready to use.

MAKES 1 CUP MUSSELS

3 pounds mussels in their shells, scrubbed, cleaned, and beards removed (see page 41)

½ cup dry white wine

½ cup Vegetable Stock (page 230)

1 clove garlic, chopped

1 small shallot, chopped

Kosher salt and freshly ground black pepper

Smoked Mussel Salad with Fennel and Marjoram

SERVES 2 AS AN APPETIZER OR LIGHT MAIN COURSE

1 cup Smoked Mussels (page 57), plus 1 tablespoon of their liquid

1 tablespoon freshly squeezed lemon juice

2 tablespoons extra-virgin olive oil

Kosher salt and freshly ground black pepper

1 small bulb fennel

2 slices sourdough bread

1 cup baby arugula

1 tablespoon minced flat-leaf parsley leaves

1 teaspoon minced fresh marjoram leaves

1 tablespoon Pickled Red Onions (page 215), drained

I love marjoram with smoked mussels. You can also use fresh tarragon or basil if you don't have marjoram. Let the shaved fennel marinate for 1 hour before you assemble the dish—it will change the texture of the fennel and also deepen its flavor. Lastly, toast the sourdough just before serving to be sure it is still warm.

In a large bowl, combine 1 tablespoon mussel cooking liquid with the lemon juice and olive oil. Season with salt and pepper and whisk to combine.

Trim the outside of the bulb of fennel to remove any blemishes and the really hard outer layer. Using a mandoline, shave the fennel very thinly until you reach the core. Discard the core.

Place the fennel slices in a large bowl with the mussel liquid mixture and toss to coat the fennel thoroughly. Refrigerate for 1 hour.

When you are ready to serve the salad, toast the sourdough slices. Remove the fennel from the fridge and add the arugula, parsley, marjoram, pickled onions, and the mussels and toss everything together; season with salt and pepper to taste. Divide the salad among two individual plates and serve the toasted sourdough on the side.

Smoked Uni Toast

This is an easy and delicious snack, but it needs to be assembled just before serving. However, you can mix the crème fraîche with the juice and zest and smoke the uni a day in advance.

Heat a grill to medium-high heat.

Brush the sourdough slices with the olive oil and grill the slices, turning occasionally, about 2 to 4 minutes total. Move the slices around the grill to help them toast evenly. (A little char is okay, but you don't want the bread overly dark.) Remove the toast from the grill and cut each slice into 4 equal pieces to make 12.

In a small bowl, combine the crème fraîche, lemon zest, and lemon juice.

Place a dollop of crème fraîche on each piece of grilled bread. Slice the Smoked Uni into 12 equal pieces and place a piece of uni on top of each dollop. Sprinkle a little sea salt on each piece of uni and garnish with a few thyme leaves.

MAKES 12 PIECES OF TOAST, 4 TO 6 SERVINGS AS AN APPETIZER

3 slices sourdough bread

2 tablespoons extra-virgin olive oil

¼ cup crème fraîche

1 teaspoon finely grated lemon zest

1 teaspoon freshly squeezed lemon juice

1 batch Smoked Uni (page 62)

Sea salt

1 teaspoon thyme leaves

Caviar Toast

Caviar has always been a luxury, but recently we've seen it become more widely available and far more approachable. This is my super easy way to enjoy it.

In a skillet large enough to hold the brioche in a single layer, melt the butter over medium heat. (If using a smaller skillet, you can do this in batches; measure out the butter accordingly.) Lightly toast the brioche in the butter on both sides and remove to a platter.

Spread a small amount of crème fraîche on each toast finger. Divide the caviar among the 12 pieces and spoon on top of the crème fraîche. Garnish with the chives and onions.

MAKES 12 PIECES, 4 TO 6 SERVINGS AS AN APPETIZER

2 tablespoons unsalted butter

12 slices brioche bread, crusts removed and cut into 1 by 2-inch rectangles

2 tablespoons crème fraîche

One 1-ounce (30-gram) tin caviar, preferably white sturgeon or osetra

1 teaspoon minced chives

1 tablespoon drained and minced Pickled Red Onions (page 215)

Smoked Uni

MAKES 2 OUNCES

2 ounces (60 grams) cleaned uni

Fresh and cleaned uni usually comes wrapped on a small wooden tray. Remove the wrapping but leave the uni on the tray while smoking. Trays are typically sold in 60-gram or 2-ounce portions.

Place the uni on its tray inside a smoking container with a tight-fitting lid or plastic wrap. Use a smoking gun to apply smoke to the container, cover, and let sit for 20 minutes. (See instructions on page 55.) Apply smoke 2 to 3 times throughout the process.

Once the uni is smoked, refrigerate until ready to use.

Classic Cold-Smoked Salmon

Classic smoked salmon is a versatile companion to so many other foods. Make sure you get a piece of salmon that has been scaled and had the pin and belly bones removed but still has the skin on. I like using a piece from the tail end of the fish. (The center or head of the filet can sometimes be too thick, which means it won't cure enough to get the correct texture.)

MAKES 25 TO 30 SLICES

2 cups Basic Cure (page 56)

One 2-pound salmon filet, skin on, bones removed

Place about ¼ cup of the cure directly in a nonreactive container or tray. Place the salmon skin-side down on top of the cure. Use the remaining cure to bury the salmon—every inch of the filet should be covered in the cure. Place the container or tray in the refrigerator and let the salmon cure for 18 to 20 hours. If liquid starts to develop around the salmon, carefully pour it off, but make sure not to brush off the cure.

Twelve hours before you want to smoke the fish, rinse it in cold water and pat dry; the fish should have a noticeably different feel and appearance to it. Place the salmon skin-side up on a clean plate or tray and refrigerate uncovered for another 6 to 10 hours—this will dry the outer flesh.

Place the salmon on a perforated tray or rack inside a smoking container with a tight-fitting lid or plastic wrap. Use a smoking gun to apply smoke to the container, cover, and let sit for 30 minutes. (See instructions on page 55.) You may want to add more smoke 2 or 3 times through the process. Once the salmon is smoked, return it to the refrigerator until chilled, about 30 minutes.

Use a long thin blade to slice the cold fish. Starting at one end of the filet, slice the fish as thinly as possible at a 45-degree angle; slice until you reach the skin but do not cut through it. Arrange the slices flat on a plate and cover with plastic wrap. Refrigerate until ready to use.

Avocado Toast with Smoked Salmon, Pickled Onions, and Sunny-Side Up Eggs

SERVES 4

4 slices sourdough bread

2 tablespoons extra-virgin olive oil

4 ripe avocados

3 tablespoons freshly squeezed lime juice

1 tablespoon sriracha hot sauce

Kosher salt and freshly ground black pepper

12 slices Classic Cold-Smoked Salmon (page 63)

½ cup Pickled Red Onions (page 215), drained

2 tablespoons canola oil

4 large eggs

1 teaspoon Aleppo pepper

This one's a brunch favorite—and will be super easy to assemble for friends if you take a few steps in advance. Make sure your avocados are ripe; I keep mine sealed in a paper bag for a few days to speed up the ripening process when needed. The pickled onions are important, too, since they help cut through the richness of the salmon and avocado. If you like heat, try adding a little more Aleppo pepper to the dish. A simple green salad is the perfect accompaniment.

Brush the sourdough with the olive oil and either grill over medium heat for a few minutes or toast in a 350°F oven for about 10 minutes.

Split the avocados in half and remove the pits. Scoop out the flesh and place in a medium mixing bowl. Add the lime juice and sriracha to the bowl and use a wooden spoon to stir until creamy. Season with salt and black pepper.

Evenly distribute the avocado mix on top of the toast slices, smoothing it out to create an even layer. Place 3 slices of smoked salmon on top of each portion and then add a few pickled onions.

Heat a medium nonstick skillet with a tight-fitting lid over medium heat. Add about ½ tablespoon of the canola oil. Add 1 egg and fry until the white is set on the bottom. Cover the skillet and cook until the white is fully set but the yolk is still runny, about 20 additional seconds. With a spatula gently transfer the cooked egg on top of one of the avocado toasts. Repeat with the remaining oil and eggs. Sprinkle a little salt and black pepper and ¼ teaspoon Aleppo pepper over each egg. Serve immediately.

Corn Pancakes with Smoked Salmon, Caviar, and Chive Crème Fraîche

I love this combination of flavors—the simple corn cakes get amped up with silky slices of smoked salmon and a kick of salt from the caviar. If you don't have fresh corn, you can substitute sliced scallions. I prefer to serve the pancakes a little warm. You can also serve them with Smoked Salmon Pâté (page 70).

In a small bowl, combine the crème fraîche and chives. Season with salt and pepper to taste and set aside.

In a large bowl, stir together the flour, cornmeal, baking soda, baking powder, and ½ teaspoon salt. In a separate, smaller bowl combine the buttermilk with the egg, corn, and melted butter. Slowly whisk the wet ingredients into the dry, mixing until they are thoroughly combined and the batter has a smooth texture. Let rest for 15 minutes.

In a medium nonstick skillet, heat about ½ tablespoon canola oil over medium heat. Spoon about ¼ cup of batter into the pan to form a 4-inch pancake. Cook until the bottom is set and bubbles are forming and popping on the surface, 3 to 4 minutes, then flip and cook for another 1 to 2 minutes. (If the pancakes are browning too quickly or too slowly, adjust the heat.) Move the finished pancake to a plate and cover with a dishtowel. Repeat the process, adding a little more oil to the pan between each pancake, until you've made 12 pancakes.

To assemble, arrange the warm pancakes on a platter in a single layer and top each with a slice of smoked salmon. Top each slice of salmon with a dollop of the chive crème fraîche and then a small spoonful of caviar.

MAKES 12 PANCAKES, 4 SERVINGS AS AN APPETIZER

½ cup crème fraîche

2 tablespoons minced chives

½ teaspoon kosher salt plus more to taste

Freshly ground black pepper

1 cup unbleached all-purpose flour

⅓ cup cornmeal

½ teaspoon baking soda

2 teaspoons baking powder

1½ cups buttermilk

1 large egg

¾ cup fresh corn kernels shaved from the cob

2 tablespoons unsalted butter, melted and cooled

2 tablespoons canola oil

12 slices Classic Cold-Smoked Salmon (page 63)

Two 1-ounce (30-gram) tins of caviar, preferably white sturgeon or osetra

Smoked Haddock

MAKES ABOUT 12 OUNCES

2 cups Basic Brine (page 56)

1½ teaspoons ground turmeric

12 ounces skinned haddock filet

Oil for baking sheet

This is my nod to Finnan haddie, a traditional cold-smoked haddock from Scotland. In the Scottish tradition, they use green wood for smoking, which produces fish that is a greenish-yellow color. The method below results in more of a yellow hue, thanks to the addition of turmeric. I like to use smoked haddock in a hash (see page 167), but you can also use this in soups, on salads, or to make a pâté similar to the Smoked Salmon or Bluefish Pâté on page 70.

In a medium saucepan, bring the brine to a boil and whisk in the turmeric; make sure it is completely combined before removing from the heat. Let the brine cool completely.

Place the haddock and brine in a large bowl where the fish is completely submerged in the brine and let sit for 15 minutes.

Preheat the oven to 250°F.

Place the haddock on a perforated tray or rack inside a smoking container with a tight-fitting lid or plastic wrap. Use a smoking gun to apply smoke to the container, cover, and let sit for 30 minutes. (See instructions on page 55.) Add a little more smoke at least 2 or 3 more times during the process. Immediately after smoking, transfer the fish to a lightly oiled baking sheet and bake in the preheated oven until cooked through, about 15 minutes. Remove and let cool.

Smoked Salmon or Bluefish

If you're using smaller pieces of fish rather than a single filet, cut back the brining time and baking time—you want the fish fully cooked but not dried out.

Cut the fish into at least 3 pieces. Place the fish and brine in a large bowl where the fish is completely submerged in the brine and refrigerate for 30 minutes. Remove the fish pieces from the brine and pat dry with paper towels.

Place the salmon or bluefish pieces on a perforated tray or rack inside a smoking container with a tight-fitting lid or plastic wrap. Use a smoking gun to apply smoke to the container, cover, and let sit for 40 minutes. (See instructions on page 55.) Add more smoke 3 or 4 times during the process.

Preheat the oven to 400° F.

Once the fish is smoked, place it on a lightly oiled baking sheet and bake in the preheated oven until the flesh is cooked through, about 8 to 12 minutes. Remove and allow to cool. Refrigerate until ready to use.

MAKES ABOUT 3 CUPS

One 1-pound salmon or bluefish filet, skinned, bones removed

2 cups Basic Brine (page 56)

Oil for baking sheet

Smoked Salmon or Bluefish Pâté

MAKES 3 CUPS

1 cup cream cheese

½ cup crème fraîche

1 tablespoon freshly squeezed lemon juice

Finely grated zest of 1 lemon

1 teaspoon chopped fresh tarragon

2 tablespoons minced red onion

½ teaspoon Tabasco sauce

1 batch Smoked Salmon or Bluefish (page 69), broken into pieces

Kosher salt and freshly ground black pepper

At the restaurant, we make a lot of pâté using any odds and ends of smoked fish. Make the pâté a day or two ahead, but be sure to pull it out of the refrigerator about 30 minutes before serving to allow it to soften a little. I always serve this with plenty of grilled bread, saltines (page 221), and pickled vegetables (page 214) on the side.

Let the cream cheese soften to room temperature. Place the cream cheese, crème fraîche, lemon juice, zest, tarragon, red onion, and Tabasco in the bowl of a stand mixer fitted with the paddle attachment. Mix on low speed until combined. Add the fish and continue mixing on low until everything just comes together—do not overmix once you've added the fish. Season to taste with salt and pepper.

Transfer the pâté to a glass jar with a lid or transfer to a serving dish and cover with plastic wrap. Refrigerate until ready to serve.

Smoked Sturgeon

MAKES 15 TO 20 SLICES

2 cups Basic Brine (page 56)

One 1-pound sturgeon filet, skin on

Oil for baking sheet

Sturgeon is highly valued for the production of its eggs, which are harvested for caviar—but it's also a great piece of fish that tastes beautiful when smoked. Most caviar and sturgeon that you'll find right now is farmed domestically. (Read more about caviar on page 98). Sturgeon flesh is really tasty, whether it's cooked as is or smoked first. Its firm, meaty texture is packed with rich flavor. Try folding together diced smoked sturgeon, shallot, tarragon, and crème fraîche for a simple seafood salad.

Place the brine in a large bowl. Add the sturgeon skin-side up. Refrigerate for 40 minutes.

Remove the fish from the brine and pat dry with paper towels. Place fish skin-side up on a plate or tray and return to the refrigerator, uncovered, until the flesh feels completely dry, 8 to 10 hours.

Place the sturgeon on a perforated tray or rack inside a smoking container with a tight-fitting lid or plastic wrap. Use a smoking gun to apply smoke to the container, cover, and let sit for 45 minutes. (See instructions on page 55.) Add a little more smoke 4 more times throughout the process. Meanwhile, preheat the oven to 250° F. Immediately after smoking, place the fish skin-side down on an oiled baking sheet and bake in the preheated oven until cooked through, about 18 minutes. Refrigerate the fish until completely cool.

Once the fish is cool, slice it by pushing a knife straight down at a 90-degree angle through the flesh, but not through the skin. Serve cold.

Smoked Boston Mackerel

Until recently, Boston mackerel wasn't a mainstream fish, but it is getting easier to find, and for good reason: Mackerel is full of flavor, plus it's inexpensive, and it's simple to work with the whole fish since they're not enormous. The meat also falls easily from the bone. Heavy smoke is important here—whole fish can take a lot of smoke flavor. I like to serve a whole smoked mackerel as part of a meal. The recipe below provides instructions for using a smoking gun and finishing the fish in the oven, but this is also a good recipe to try on your outdoor grill. Sample it both ways and see which you prefer. See page 151 for more information on cleaning whole fish.

Place the brine and fish in a large bowl where the fish are completely submerged in the brine. Refrigerate for about 40 minutes.

Remove the fish from the brine and pat dry with paper towels. Place the fish on a plate or tray and return to the refrigerator, uncovered, for 2 hours—this will completely dry the fish.

Place the fish on a perforated tray or rack inside a smoking container with a tight-fitting lid or plastic wrap. Use a smoking gun to apply smoke to the container, cover, and let sit for 45 minutes. (See instructions on page 55.) Add more smoke 4 or 5 additional times throughout the process to create heavy smoke. Meanwhile, preheat the oven to 400° F.

Immediately after smoking, place the fish on a lightly oiled baking sheet and bake in the preheated oven until the flesh is opaque and flakes easily, about 12 to 15 minutes. Remove and let cool.

When you're ready to use the smoked mackerel, remove the skin and carefully pick the flesh from the bones.

MAKES 4 WHOLE SMOKED FISH

3 cups Basic Brine (page 56)

4 whole mackerel, 10 to 12 ounces each, with heads, cleaned and gutted

Oil for baking sheet

Smoked Mackerel Salad with Oranges, Walnut Pesto, and Frisée

SERVES 4

2 slices rye bread, cut into 1-inch squares

¼ cup extra-virgin olive oil

1 Smoked Boston Mackerel (page 73)

2 oranges, cut into segments (see note opposite)

2 cups frisée lettuce

¼ cup flat-leaf parsley leaves

¼ cup Pickled Red Onions (page 215), drained

1 tablespoon freshly squeezed lemon juice

Kosher salt and freshly ground black pepper

1 cup Walnut Pesto (page 223)

You can assemble this salad with almost any hot-smoked fish, but I personally love it with mackerel. When you're ready to put it all together, make sure the pesto is at room temperature so that it spreads easily. I like a good rye bread for the croutons, but you can use sourdough or wheat bread, too—or skip the croutons and serve the salad with slices of grilled bread.

Preheat the oven to 350°F.

On a rimmed baking sheet, toss the rye bread squares with 2 tablespoons olive oil. Toast in the oven until crispy, about 8 minutes.

Remove the flesh from the smoked mackerel, being careful to avoid getting any bones or skin mixed in. Break up the pieces by hand (it should be about ½ cup) and place in a large mixing bowl. Add the orange segments, frisée, parsley, and pickled onions to the bowl, then add the lemon juice and remaining 2 tablespoons olive oil. Season with salt and pepper. Toss gently to combine.

To serve, spread the pesto on the bottom of a serving plate and build the salad on top of the pesto. Top with the rye croutons and serve.

How to Section an Orange

Every cook should know how to section, or supreme, citrus. Beautifully sectioned fruit makes a dish look amazing. Use a small, sharp serrated knife.

Cut the ends off the top and bottom of the orange, being sure to make a straight, even cut that exposes enough of the orange that you can see the sections. The cut needs to be even so that the orange sits flat on a cutting board.

Remove a section of the rind from top to bottom, following the contour of the orange. Repeat this all around the orange. When done, the orange should look like the rind fell off; no flat sides or white pith should be left.

Pick up the orange and hold it over a bowl with a strainer set over it to reserve the juice. Carefully cut on either side of the white membranes that separate each orange section. Remove each segment and squeeze the remaining part of the orange over the strainer to collect every drop of juice.

Smoked and Grilled Scallops

1 pound sea scallops

2 cups Basic Brine (page 56)

2 tablespoons canola oil

What I love about scallops is that they don't require much in terms of preparation and really retain their flavor when smoked. I recommend smoking the scallops a day in advance and then finishing them on the grill right before you're ready to serve them. I like to slice scallops into thin rounds and finish them with a little sea salt before serving them at room temperature.

Remove the foot from each scallop. Place the scallops and brine in a bowl where the scallops are completely submerged in the brine. Refrigerate for 30 minutes. Remove the scallops from the brine and pat dry with a paper towel. Place the scallops on a plate or tray in the refrigerator and let dry for about 8 hours.

Place the scallops on a perforated tray or rack inside a smoking container with a tight-fitting lid or plastic wrap. Use a smoking gun to apply smoke to the container, cover, and let sit for 15 minutes. (See instructions on page 55.) You may want to add a little more smoke halfway through the process. Return the scallops to the refrigerator until chilled, about 30 minutes.

To finish the process, preheat a grill to medium heat. Rub canola oil onto each scallop. Grill the scallops until just seared and warmed through, about 2 minutes per side.

Smoked Trout

Smoked trout is another classic preparation that is both delicious and versatile. In this recipe, we cold-smoke and bake the fish, but you can also put the fish on a hot grill after smoking them. Trout usually are sold whole or butterflied (i.e., left whole but slit down the belly, cleaned, and with the bones removed). Butterflied trout are a little easier to handle, as the meat separates from the skin more readily. If the fish don't completely fit into the smoking container, remove the heads.

Place the brine and trout in a large bowl where the fish is completely submerged in the brine. Refrigerate and let soak for 45 minutes.

Remove the fish from the brine and pat dry with paper towels. If using butterflied trout, spread the fish open and place on a plate or tray, flesh side up. Refrigerate for 2 to 3 hours so that the meat completely dries. If the trout aren't butterflied, make sure the cavity of each trout is patted as dry as possible before refrigerating.

Preheat the oven to 250° F.

Place the whole trout on a perforated tray or rack inside a smoking container with a tight-fitting lid or plastic wrap. Use a smoking gun to apply smoke to the container, cover, and let sit for 40 minutes. (See instructions on page 55.) Add smoke 4 or 5 more times throughout the process. Immediately after smoking, place the fish on a lightly oiled baking sheet and bake in the preheated oven for 12 minutes if butterflied, 20 minutes if whole. Let cool completely before removing the meat from the skin; make sure all pin and other bones are removed as well. Refrigerate meat until ready to use.

MAKES 2 WHOLE SMOKED FISH

3 cups Basic Brine (page 56)

2 whole trout, 14 to 18 ounces each, preferably butterflied

Oil for baking sheet

How to Build a Smoked and Cured Board

ON THE BOARD

(clockwise from the upper left)

Smoked Bluefish Pâté

Smoked Salmon Pâté

Classic Salmon Gravlax

Classic Cold-Smoked Salmon

Smoked Boston Mackerel

Pickled Vegetables

Smoked Mussels

Smoked and Grilled Scallops

Smoked Trout

Beet-Cured Steelhead Trout

Pickled Red Onions

TO SERVE

Grilled sourdough bread

For me, there might be no better seafood-focused meal than a platter of oysters and a board brimming with smoked and cured seafood. It might seem difficult to imagine setting out a platter of twelve different smoked and cured seafoods for a weekend dinner party—but it's not as hard as you think. Planning ahead is essential. And don't reach too far for your first and second try. Putting two or three well-executed items together is going to be better than rushing to get six elements on the board.

First, think ahead by at least a few days. Curing seafood, such as gravlax and smoked salmon, takes time, while some of the hot-smoked recipes can be done the same day with a quick brine and smoke.

Start by prepping the pâtés, which can be made a couple of days in advance, and at the same time, cure a few items for cold smoking, such as the Classic Cold-Smoked Salmon (page 63) and Beet-Cured Steelhead Trout (page 81). Once those have been cured and you've set up your smoking equipment, it's easy to smoke several dishes back-to-back.

Brine and smoke things like scallops and mackerel ahead of time, but wait to cook them until right before you're ready to serve.

I use a lot of grilled bread in this cookbook as it makes for a simple but needed accompaniment to many of these dishes. Mostly, I refer to sourdough but any good bread will do. Grilled baguette or rye are two more of my go-to favorites. You can also go with saltines (page 221) or store-bought crackers instead of, or in addition to, grilled bread.

Lastly, if you've got the time and energy, add a few homemade pickled items. Or, make it easier on yourself and buy a few quality pickled items at the store.

Beet-Cured Steelhead Trout

You can really taste the flavor of the beets in this dish—plus, the color of the beets makes this a beautiful dish to serve. If you can't find steelhead trout, you can use arctic char or salmon. Buy a whole filet that's been scaled but with the skin left on and with the pin and belly bones removed. Use a box grater to grate the beet (peel it first), and don't squeeze the juice from the grated pieces.

Place a large piece of plastic wrap on a plate or tray; make sure there is enough wrap to cover the entire filet. Place about 1 cup of cure on the plastic wrap. Place the filet skin-side down on top of the cure and then top the filet with the grated beet. Sprinkle the tarragon over the beets. Finish by covering with the remaining cure. The entire fish should be covered in the cure and beet mixture. Fold the plastic wrap around the fish to hold everything together. Place the plate or tray in the refrigerator and let cure for 24 to 36 hours.

Remove the plate or tray, unwrap the fish, and rinse the filet under cold water. Pat dry with paper towels and thinly slice at a 45-degree angle. Be sure to cut down to, but not through, the skin.

MAKES 20 TO 25 SLICES

3 cups Basic Cure (page 56)

One 1½- to 2-pound steelhead trout filet, skin on

1 cup grated red beet

2 tablespoons chopped fresh tarragon

Classic Salmon Gravlax

3 cups Basic Cure (page 56)

One 2-pound salmon filet, skin on

2 tablespoons chopped dill

Finely grated zest of 1 lemon

Making your own gravlax, or lox, takes time, but it's an easy recipe and should become part of your rotation, especially since the end result can (and should) be part of any meal.

Place a large piece of plastic wrap on a plate or tray; make sure there is enough wrap to cover the entire filet. Spread 1 cup of the cure in the center of the plastic wrap; loosely shape the cure so that it's the same shape as the filet. Place the salmon skin-side down on top of the cure. Rub the dill and the lemon zest over the flesh of the filet. Pour the remaining cure over the filet so that it completely covers the flesh (see page 52).

Wrap the plastic tightly around the salmon filet. Place the plate in the refrigerator and let cure for 24 to 30 hours. Unwrap the filet and rinse under cold water. Pat dry. To serve, use a long thin blade to slice the cold fish. Starting at one end of the filet, slice the fish as thinly as possible at a 45-degree angle; slice until you reach the skin but do not cut through it. Lay the slices flat on a platter (they can be overlapping) and refrigerate until ready to serve.

Coriander-Cured Spanish Mackerel

MAKES 15 TO 20 SLICES

1 teaspoon whole coriander seeds

2 cups Basic Cure (page 56)

One 12- to 16-ounce Spanish mackerel filet, skin on

Spanish mackerel is one of my favorites for curing and smoking. Spanish mackerel is slightly larger than Boston mackerel and a little leaner, but it has great texture. It's also a fairly inexpensive fish, so this is a great recipe for getting the best bang for your buck. When buying the fish, make sure the filet is in good condition with no gaps in the flesh. Ask for it to be skin on with all bones removed. The end result is a little salty, but the cure gives it an amazing texture—just make sure to slice it really thinly.

In a dry sauté pan, toast the coriander seeds over medium heat. Gently shake the pan until you can smell the toasted spice. Remove the pan from the heat and place the coriander in a spice grinder. Pulse until finely ground; remove and discard any large pieces.

Place a large piece of plastic wrap on a plate or tray; make sure there is enough wrap to cover the entire filet. Mix half of the ground coriander with the cure and place about ½ cup of the mixture on the plastic wrap. Arrange the filet skin-side down on top of the cure. Sprinkle the other half of the ground coriander over the mackerel filet, taking care to coat the sides. Arrange the remaining cure on the fish. Wrap the plastic completely around the fish and place the plate or tray in the refrigerator. Let cure for about 24 hours.

Once the fish is cured, remove the plate or tray from the refrigerator, unwrap the fish, and rinse under cold water. Pat dry with paper towels. To serve, thinly slice at a 45-degree angle, making sure to slice down to, but not through, the skin.

Rosemary and Black Pepper–Cured Tuna

The cut of the tuna is important for this recipe. You need a nice, evenly cut piece of tuna that is longer than it is thick. I recommend reaching out to your fishmonger to make a request—they should be able to do it with a few days' notice. Ask for a piece that's about 3 inches wide and 10 to 12 inches long. A standard tuna steak will also work, but you'll need to cut back on the cure time.

Place the peppercorns in a dry sauté pan over medium heat and toast, moving the pan constantly, until fragrant. Remove the peppercorns from the heat and grind finely in a spice grinder. In a bowl, combine the ground pepper with the rosemary and the cure.

Sprinkle the cure mixture over the surface of a tray or large plate. Roll the tuna through the cure so that it covers all sides; use your hands to sprinkle more cure over any bare spots. Gently shake off any excess cure that does not stick to the tuna. Wrap the tuna tightly in plastic wrap and refrigerate for 10 to 12 hours.

Unwrap the tuna, rinse under cold water, and pat dry. Rub the olive oil all over the surface of the tuna. To serve, slice thinly, cutting at a 90-degree angle.

MAKES 25 TO 30 SLICES

1 teaspoon whole black peppercorns

1 teaspoon minced rosemary leaves

½ cup Basic Cure (page 56)

One 12-ounce piece tuna, 2 inches wide by 6 inches long, skinned

2 tablespoons extra-virgin olive oil

Tuna Crudo with Ginger and Black Garlic Aïoli

SERVES 4 AS AN APPETIZER

12 ounces trimmed tuna loin

¼ cup Black Garlic Aïoli
(page 225)

1 ripe avocado

2 tablespoons Ginger Vinegar
(page 228)

1 tablespoon freshly squeezed
lime juice

Sea salt

1 cup Crispy Shallots (page 213)

2 teaspoons picked chervil leaves

This is easily one of our most popular dishes at Row 34. Black garlic is aged for several weeks in controlled conditions. It takes on a fermented odor and a unique, slightly sweet flavor that balances nicely with the ginger and the tuna. (You can find black garlic at specialty markets or online.) Look for a uniform rectangular piece of tuna, or trim the loin to create a rectangular log. You can use any leftover trimmings to make the tuna tartare on page 102.

Slice the tuna into 16 thin slices. Place on a plate in a single layer and refrigerate.

Spread the aïoli down the center of a serving platter in an even line.

Cut the avocado in half and remove the pit. Slice the avocado and arrange the slices on top of the aïoli in an even layer.

In a small bowl, combine 1 tablespoon of the vinegar with the lime juice. Pull the tuna slices from the fridge and pour the mixture over the slices, gently turning the pieces so that the mixture coats all sides of the tuna. Let the tuna sit for 15 seconds.

Remove the tuna from the liquid and loosely roll the tuna slices into small cylinders. Place the cylinders on top of the avocado slices. Drizzle the remaining 1 tablespoon vinegar over the tuna. Season each tuna cylinder with a few flakes of sea salt and garnish with the shallots and chervil.

Steelhead Crudo with Radishes and Black Rice

Steelhead trout is a farm-raised fish that is in the same family as salmon and standard trout. It tastes like a cross between the two. Steelhead is fairly rich, so it marries well with other strong flavors. If you can't find steelhead, you can use farmed or wild salmon as a substitute. While I call for watermelon radishes and breakfast radishes in this recipe, feel free to replace them with your own favorites. Also, you'll have a little leftover cooked rice for other uses.

Place the fish on a cutting board and starting at the tail end, slice the filet into thin pieces, keeping the knife at a 45-degree angle. Each slice should be 2 to 3 inches in length. Place slices on a plate or platter and refrigerate until you're ready to assemble the dish.

In a small bowl, whisk together the lime juice, sriracha, sesame oil, and olive oil. Refrigerate until ready to use.

In a small saucepan with a lid, combine the rice and stock. Bring to a boil, then lower the heat and simmer until the rice is tender, about 20 minutes. Drain the rice and spread it on a baking sheet to cool; season with salt and pepper.

Peel and seed the cucumber and dice into ¼-inch pieces. Place the cucumber in a bowl with the watermelon and breakfast radishes. Add 2 tablespoons of the cooked black rice to the bowl and pour about half of the lime dressing over the mixture, then toss to combine. Season to taste with salt and pepper.

To serve, on a chilled platter, arrange the steelhead slices in a circle, overlapping slightly. Drizzle the remaining lime dressing over the fish and season with salt and pepper. Spoon the cucumber mixture in the center of the circle. Garnish with the arugula leaves and sesame seeds and serve at once.

SERVES 4 AS AN APPETIZER

One 10-ounce skinned steelhead trout filet

2 tablespoons freshly squeezed lime juice

1 teaspoon sriracha hot sauce

1 tablespoon sesame oil

1 tablespoon extra-virgin olive oil

¼ cup black rice, rinsed

1¼ cups Vegetable Stock (page 230)

Kosher salt and freshly ground black pepper

1 English cucumber

8 thin slices peeled watermelon radish, cut into quarters

2 breakfast radishes, thinly sliced

¼ cup baby arugula

1 teaspoon sesame seeds, toasted

Fluke Crudo with Lemon Oil, Charred Scallions, and Pistachios

SERVES 4 AS AN APPETIZER

1 bunch scallions

1 tablespoon canola oil

¼ cup shelled pistachios, lightly
    toasted and chopped

2 tablespoons Ginger Vinegar
    (page 228)

Kosher salt and freshly ground
    black pepper

One 12-ounce skinned fluke filet,
    about 2 inches wide

1 tablespoon Lemon Oil (opposite)

Sea salt

Fluke is one of my favorite fish for making crudo. It slices neatly and leaves little to no trim left over. The other component of this dish that I love is the charred scallions. Be careful charring them: You want the pan to be really hot so that the scallions get some color on the outside but don't cook to a mushy texture. The charring happens fast, so be ready. The lemon oil recipe makes more than you need, but it is a great item to have in the refrigerator, where it will keep for several weeks. I use it in all sorts of recipes, and it works well with most fish.

Cut the bunch of scallions in half, separating the white parts from the green. Remove and discard the root ends from the white parts and reserve the green parts. In a medium sauté pan, heat the canola oil over high heat. Add the scallion whites to the pan and cook, turning every minute or so, until the outsides start to darken; move quickly so that the scallion whites do not get too soft.

Once charred, remove the scallions from the pan and let sit until cool enough to handle. Slice the scallions thinly and place them in a medium-sized bowl. Add the pistachios and 1 tablespoon vinegar. Season with salt and pepper to taste.

Starting at the tail end of the fluke filet, make very thin slices at a 45-degree angle. Loosely fold the fluke slices and place them on a chilled serving plate in several rows in a single layer. Sprinkle the scallion-pistachio mix around the fluke. Drizzle the fish with the lemon oil and the remaining 1 tablespoon vinegar. Slice the scallion greens very thinly on an angle and scatter over the fish. Season each piece of fluke with a pinch of sea salt and serve.

Lemon Oil

In a medium saucepan with a tight-fitting lid, combine the olive oil with the peppercorns, mustard seeds, thyme, and lemon zest. Heat the oil to 160° F, then cover the pan, remove from heat, and allow it to cool and rest at room temperature for 8 hours. Strain the oil mixture through a fine-mesh strainer, remove and discard the solids, and transfer the oil to a clean, airtight container. Refrigerate until ready to use.

FOR THE LEMON OIL

MAKES ABOUT ¼ CUP

¼ cup extra-virgin olive oil

½ teaspoon whole black peppercorns

½ teaspoon mustard seeds

1 sprig thyme

2 wide strips lemon zest

Scallop Ceviche with Cilantro Pesto

SERVES 4 AS AN APPETIZER

1 pound sea scallops, cut into
small dice

3 tablespoons freshly squeezed
lime juice

About 2 tablespoons Cilantro
Pesto (page 223)

2 oranges, cut into segments and
diced (see note on page 75)

6 cilantro leaves

1 tablespoon Pickled Red Onions,
drained and diced (page 215)

Sea salt

Sweet Potato or Taro Chips
(page 216)

clockwise from top right:
Vegetable Chips, page 216
Acadian Redfish Ceviche with Roasted
Jalapeño and Lime, page 94
Scallop Ceviche with Cilantro Pesto,
this page
Striped Bass Ceviche with Grilled Corn
and Fresno Pepper, page 95

I love scallop ceviche, mainly because of the texture and flavor of the scallops, which stand up to bold ingredients like cilantro. If you're feeling brave, buy live sea scallops in the shell and shuck them yourself. The pesto can be made in advance; this will yield more than you need, but it freezes well for another use.

In a medium bowl, mix together the scallops and the lime juice. Let sit for 5 minutes, stirring occasionally. The scallops will start to change color and firm up. Pour off any excess liquid from the scallops, then add the pesto a little at a time, tossing gently to combine between additions, until the scallops are well coated but not swimming in pesto.

Once the scallops are coated, arrange the ceviche in a serving dish and garnish with the orange segments, cilantro leaves, and onions. Season with sea salt. Serve the chips on the side.

Acadian Redfish Ceviche with Roasted Jalapeño and Lime

SERVES 4 AS AN APPETIZER

1 teaspoon canola oil

1 large jalapeño pepper

One 12-ounce skinned redfish filet

3 tablespoons freshly squeezed
    lime juice

1 tablespoon chopped cilantro

½ cup peeled, seeded, and diced
    English cucumber

Kosher salt

2 tablespoons extra-virgin olive
    oil

Taro Chips (page 216)

Acadian redfish are little orange-colored fish caught off the East Coast, usually in deeper waters. When I was young, the only time I saw them was when they were being used for lobster bait. But as we've put pressure on other ocean species, we've learned that redfish are delicious, and they've now found their way onto our plates. That said, this recipe will also work with scallops, fluke, halibut, or bass. Be sure to wear gloves while working with jalapeño peppers.

Preheat the oven to 500° F (or use a toaster oven).

Brush the canola oil on the outside of the jalapeño pepper and place the pepper on a baking sheet. Roast until slightly charred, 5 to 7 minutes. Remove and place the pepper in a bowl, cover tightly with plastic wrap, and let the pepper steam for 10 minutes. Wearing gloves, use the back of a paring knife to scrape the skin off the pepper. Cut the pepper in half lengthwise and remove the seeds and stem. Cut the pepper into a small dice.

Dice the redfish filet into ¼-inch pieces and place in a large bowl. Add the diced jalapeño, lime juice, cilantro, and cucumber. Toss all of the ingredients together and season with salt. Refrigerate for about 10 minutes.

To serve, transfer the ceviche to a serving dish and drizzle the olive oil over top. Serve with chips on the side.

Striped Bass Ceviche with Grilled Corn and Fresno Pepper

Striped bass is a summertime staple along the East Coast—my staff and I have caught a few ourselves over the years. I like striped bass for ceviche because it maintains a firm texture. Request the thick end of the filet near the head for optimal results. You can serve this over a green salad as a great way to start a meal or even as the meal itself. A note: I intentionally left ground pepper out of the recipe since the Fresno gives it all the peppery kick it needs.

Dice the bass filet into ¼-inch pieces. Place in a large bowl and refrigerate until ready to assemble.

Heat a grill to medium-high heat.

Brush the ear of corn with the canola oil and sprinkle with a little salt. Grill the corn, turning frequently, until the entire cob is lightly charred. Set aside. Once the corn is cool enough to handle, shave the kernels from the cob.

Split the Fresno pepper in half lengthwise and remove the stem and seeds. Place the pepper skin-side-down on the cutting board (it's easier to cut through the inside of a pepper) and cut into thin strips, then mince the strips into small pieces.

Remove the striped bass from the refrigerator. Add the lime juice and season with salt. Toss to combine and return the bowl to the refrigerator for 20 minutes.

When ready to serve, add the charred corn, the minced Fresno pepper, the red onion, the cucumber, and the cilantro to the bowl with the striped bass. Gently toss to combine. Place the ceviche in a serving bowl and drizzle the olive oil on top. Serve chips on the side.

SERVES 4 AS AN APPETIZER

One 12-ounce skinned striped bass filet

1 ear corn, husked and silks removed

1 teaspoon canola oil

Kosher salt

1 small Fresno pepper

3 tablespoons freshly squeezed lime juice

2 tablespoons minced red onion

¼ cup peeled, seeded, and diced English cucumber

1 tablespoon chopped cilantro

2 tablespoons extra-virgin olive oil

Plantain Chips (page 216)

Salmon Belly Poke with Brown Rice, Avocado, Cucumber, Ginger, and Radish

Salmon belly is the flavorful cut from the bottom of the filet. To get the freshest piece available, call your local fish market to request the cut. Buy the mango and avocado a few days in advance and let them ripen. Be sure the rice you're using is warm, not hot. The soy sauce is naturally salty, so taste before adding more seasoning to the bowls.

In a medium saucepan, combine the stock and the brown rice. Season with salt. Bring to a boil, reduce the heat to a simmer, and cover. Simmer until the rice is tender, about 20 minutes. Remove the pan from the heat, keeping the pan covered until ready to use.

Peel the mango and remove the flesh from the pit; dice into ¼-inch pieces. Split the avocado in half and remove the pit; slice the avocado into thin slices from top to bottom. Scoop out the avocado slices using a large spoon.

Place the warm rice in a bowl and toss with half of the dressing. Season with salt and pepper. Divide the rice among 4 serving bowls; divide the mango, avocado, cucumber, carrot, and radish between the bowls, making small separate piles of each ingredient on top of the rice.

In a medium bowl, carefully stir together the salmon belly with half of the remaining dressing. Season with salt and pepper. Divide evenly among the 4 bowls. Garnish each bowl with a pinch each of black sesame seeds and togarashi (if using) and a few sliced scallions. Drizzle the remaining dressing over the top of each bowl and serve immediately.

Soy Ginger Dressing

In a small bowl, whisk together all of the ingredients. Set aside at room temperature.

SERVES 4 AS AN APPETIZER

2 cups Vegetable Stock (page 230)

1 cup short-grain brown rice

Kosher salt

1 ripe mango

1 ripe avocado

½ cup Soy Ginger Dressing (see below)

Freshly ground black pepper

1 cup peeled, seeded, and diced English cucumber

¼ cup thinly sliced carrot

1 red radish, thinly sliced

One 12-ounce piece salmon belly, boned, skinned, and cut into ¼-inch dice

1 teaspoon black sesame seeds

¼ teaspoon togarashi powder (optional)

2 scallions, thinly sliced

FOR THE SOY GINGER DRESSING

MAKES ABOUT ½ CUP

¼ cup soy sauce

1 tablespoon sesame oil

2 tablespoons freshly squeezed lime juice

2 tablespoons sriracha hot sauce

2 teaspoons rice wine vinegar

1 teaspoon grated ginger (use a microplane)

Caviar 101

For too long, caviar was seen as a luxury product—much of it was imported and harvested from wild fish stocks, making it an expensive delicacy. But several recent changes in the world of caviar have made it more accessible, less expensive, and more widely available. Yes, really good caviar is still an investment, but for special occasions, or even elevated everyday snacks, consider reaching for a tin of good caviar.

Caviar is defined as fish eggs that are harvested from the sturgeon family of fish and then salt-cured. There is also fish roe, or eggs, from paddle-fish or other species that is not technically caviar. This is typically less expensive than true caviar, yet it provides the same salty, nuanced kick.

Caviar is differentiated by the specific species of sturgeon it comes from. You might find labels like white sturgeon, osetra, beluga, and sevruga. I tend to lean toward white sturgeon and osetra, which are both available from U.S. producers.

Most caviar sold in the United States is either imported or harvested and packed domestically. In the past, caviar was harvested from wild fish populations in the Black and Caspian Seas, but overfishing depleted those populations. Now, the United States has a ban on selling or harvesting wild sturgeon, meaning you'll only find farmed caviar in the United States. While imported caviar can be very pricey, American caviar is increasingly a better choice for quality, price, and environmental reasons. Our own domestic farmed options are growing, with operations like Sterling in California and Marshallberg Farm in North Carolina leading the charge.

As for what you'll taste, the small rounded beads range in texture, flavor, color, and size. The beads might be firm with a distinct pop or run a little smoother and soften on the tongue. They might be glistening black, deep green, or brownish in hue, and the flavors can range from buttery, earthy, and nutty to bright and loaded with umami. All caviar and roe will have a distinctly salty punch.

I'm intrigued by the strong connection oysters and caviar share. They're similar in that both are products that were once overfished or overconsumed and now their respective industries have been revived through farming. Both are great domestic products that have overcome their pasts. And just as oysters are having their moment, American caviar is on the rise.

These are the three caviars we use most frequently at Row 34:

Sterling white sturgeon is the Kumamoto oyster of caviar, a flavor bomb that can taste like Parmesan, moss, and fish oil all at once. Sterling harvests its caviar in California and sells it at three different grades. We get a mid-tier grade that's both stunning and not overly expensive.

Marshallberg osetra has slightly bigger beads that can be green-gold in color. Grown in North Carolina, this style is much lighter and far less oily than white sturgeon. You'll get a more subtle, balanced, and buttery finish.

Wild paddlefish roe is salt-cured fish eggs but doesn't count as caviar since it's not harvested from sturgeon. Still, these eggs are interesting—

and the right price for everyday snacking. They're harvested from a monitored wild population in Oklahoma. A little more savory and delicate, these don't hit you over the head with salt, and the small beads are a little less oily than other styles.

How to Keep, Store, and Eat Caviar

Keep caviar and roe tins in the refrigerator, set on top of a bowl of ice—ideally caviar should stay around 38°F. Kept that way, unopened tins can last three to four weeks. Once a tin has been opened, it will only last a couple of days. When tasting caviar, avoid using a metal spoon, as metal can react with the fish oil. Instead, use a neutral surface—mother of pearl is the most popular tasting tool, but you can also use a plastic spoon to put a small pile of caviar onto the fleshy part of your hand between your wrist and your thumb. Eat it right off your skin (called a "caviar bump") to get the cleanest expression. Of course, caviar adds an extra bit of luxury to most delicate savory dishes. We add caviar to deviled eggs (page 108) and poached oysters (page 45) and feature it in our Caviar Toast (page 61).

CHAPTER THREE

Row 34 Favorites

Tuna Tartare with Sweet Potato Chips

10 ounces tuna, diced into ¼-inch cubes

½ English cucumber, peeled, seeded, and cut into ¼-inch dice

¼ cup minced red onion

3 tablespoons freshly squeezed lemon juice

2 tablespoons sesame oil

1 tablespoon sriracha hot sauce

Kosher salt

1 tablespoon minced chives

2 teaspoons toasted sesame seeds

1 batch Sweet Potato Chips (page 216)

Tuna tartare is one of those great recipes to have in your repertoire—easy to assemble and terrific to share. Of course, when it comes to raw fish, you want the freshest you can find and always keep it cold. If you buy a piece of tuna with the skin on, use a spoon to scrape any meat off the skin and fold that into the diced tuna. And be sure to mix the tartare right before serving, as the acid from the lemon juice will change the texture and color of the fish as it sits.

In a medium bowl, combine the tuna, cucumber, onion, lemon juice, sesame oil, and sriracha. Season with salt and place in a serving dish. Garnish with the minced chives and sesame seeds. Serve immediately with chips on the side.

Shrimp Cocktail

There is nothing particularly local or seasonal about most shrimp. While there are some good wild options that are harvested in the United States, most of the shrimp consumed domestically is grown overseas. Indeed, shrimp is our country's number one imported seafood. For shrimp cocktail, I like using shrimp labeled U12. When shrimp are labeled with a number, it usually refers to the quantity per pound, so if you see 21/25, it means there are 21 to 25 shrimp per pound. There are only a dozen U12 shrimp per pound—the larger shrimp make the presentation feel special.

Peel the shrimp down to the last section of the shell closest to the tail, leaving that part of the shell intact. Use a paring knife to split the backs of the shrimp and remove the veins. Rinse the shrimp under cold water.

Prepare a bowl of ice water. In a large saucepan, combine 3 quarts water, the lemon, and the salt and bring to a boil. Meanwhile, place the bay leaf, peppercorns, thyme, and rosemary in a coffee filter or a piece of cheesecloth and use kitchen twine to tie the top together to make a pouch; add to the water. Lower the heat so that the water is simmering. Add the shrimp, adjusting the heat to keep the water at a simmer. Cook the shrimp for 5 minutes, then use a slotted spoon to scoop them from the simmering water and transfer them to the ice water. Let the shrimp cool for 6 minutes, then remove from the water and drain.

To serve, place the cocktail sauce in a medium bowl or serving dish and arrange the shrimp around the perimeter of the bowl, hanging over the rim.

MAKES 12 SHRIMP, 2 TO 4 APPETIZER SERVINGS

12 large shell-on shrimp, about 1 pound

½ lemon

2 tablespoons kosher salt

1 bay leaf

6 whole peppercorns

2 sprigs thyme

1 sprig rosemary

½ cup Cocktail Sauce (page 33)

Fried Calamari with Spicy Aïoli

There's a reason fried calamari is such a popular dish—it can be delicious when done right. The flavor of squid meat is pretty neutral, meaning it marries easily with many other flavors. And when handled correctly the texture is light and just barely chewy. Try to find squid that's been caught and cleaned domestically. If you live in an area where calamari are fished, buy it in season and clean it yourself. It's a small amount of work for big reward. For more tips on frying at home, see Frying Seafood at Home (page 15).

Cut the calamari tubes into ¼-inch rounds. In a medium bowl, combine the calamari rounds and tentacles, pepper, and red onion with the buttermilk and sriracha. Stir well to coat. Refrigerate for 30 minutes.

Line a plate with paper towels. Place the oil in a straight-sided skillet or Dutch oven and heat it to 350°F. Drain the calamari and vegetables, discarding the buttermilk. Place the seasoned flour in a clean bowl and add the calamari and vegetables, tossing well to coat each piece. Make sure the pieces aren't sticking together.

Place the floured calamari in a fry basket, shaking off any excess flour as you transfer them. Carefully lower the basket into the hot oil. Fry until every piece is light brown and crisp, about 2 to 3 minutes. Remove the basket and turn the calamari out onto the prepared plate to drain. (If you don't have a fry basket, shake off the excess flour from the calamari and carefully place the floured calamari directly into the oil. Once fried, use a slotted spoon or skimmer to transfer the calamari to the paper towel–lined plate.)

Season immediately with salt. To serve, spread the calamari out on a platter and garnish with the parsley and lemon wedges. Serve the aïoli on the side.

SERVES 4 AS AN APPETIZER

1 pound cleaned calamari, tubes and tentacles

1 Fresno or jalapeño pepper, seeded and sliced into thin rounds

¼ cup thinly sliced red onion

½ cup buttermilk

1 tablespoon sriracha hot sauce

4 cups canola oil for frying

3 cups Seasoned Flour (page 229)

Sea salt

2 tablespoons roughly chopped flat-leaf parsley leaves

4 lemon wedges (see page 43)

½ cup Spicy Aïoli (page 225)

Crab Cakes with Fennel and Apple Salad

MAKES 6 CRAB CAKES

1 pound crab meat

2 scallions, white and green parts thinly sliced

1 tablespoon Dijon mustard

1 tablespoon chopped flat-leaf parsley leaves

¼ cup mayonnaise

¾ cup panko breadcrumbs

2 teaspoons Tabasco sauce

Finely grated zest and juice of 1 lemon

Kosher salt and freshly ground black pepper

¼ cup canola oil

¾ cup Horseradish Aïoli (page 224)

2½ cups Fennel and Apple Salad (opposite)

When shopping for crabmeat, you'll find a lot of different options available, and while fresh is always best, there are some pasteurized crab meats at the market that are pretty good. If the meat has a lot of moisture, I recommend draining it or wrapping it in a dish towel and wringing out the excess water. These crab cakes can be seared in advance and warmed up in the oven just before serving. The sweetness of the crab and the apple are a great balance to the horseradish—and if horseradish aïoli is not your thing, try a more straightforward aïoli instead—there are lots of options on pages 224–225. Wait to make the salad until just before serving.

Spread the crabmeat out on a tray so you can inspect it for shells. Once any shells have been removed, place the crab meat in a medium bowl and add the scallions, mustard, parsley, mayonnaise, ½ cup of the panko breadcrumbs, Tabasco, lemon zest, and lemon juice. Season with salt and pepper. Stir the ingredients until well combined, trying not to break up the crabmeat too much; large, intact pieces of crab are what you want.

Divide the mixture into 6 equal balls. Spread the remaining ¼ cup panko on a large plate and press one crabmeat ball into the panko, using your hand to flatten it into a cake. Flip the cake to coat both sides with the panko. Set aside and repeat with remaining crabmeat and the panko.

Line a plate with paper towels. In a straight-sided skillet or Dutch oven, heat the canola oil over medium-high heat. Once the oil is hot, fry the cakes, turning once, until golden brown, about 3 minutes per side. Lower the temperature as needed so that it doesn't burn the exterior of the crab cakes, and work in batches if necessary to avoid crowding the pan. As the crab cakes are finished, use a slotted spoon or spatula to transfer them gently to the prepared plate.

To serve: Spread the aïoli in the center of a serving platter. Place the salad on top of the aïoli and top the salad with the crab cakes.

Fennel and Apple Salad

Core, quarter, and thinly slice the apple. In a large bowl, toss the apple slices with the fennel, arugula, lemon juice, and olive oil. Season with salt and pepper, then plate the dish.

FOR THE FENNEL AND APPLE SALAD

MAKES ABOUT 2½ CUPS

1 large apple

1 cup shaved fennel

1 cup arugula

1 tablespoon freshly squeezed lemon juice

2 tablespoons extra-virgin olive oil

Kosher salt and freshly ground black pepper

Deviled Eggs with Smoked Salmon and Caviar

MAKES 12 EGG HALVES, 4 TO 6 SERVINGS

6 large eggs

¼ cup Aïoli (page 224)

1 teaspoon Dijon mustard

1 teaspoon apple cider vinegar

Kosher salt and freshly ground black pepper

12 (1 by 1-inch) pieces Classic Cold-Smoked Salmon (page 63)

1 ounce caviar, preferably white sturgeon or osetra

1 tablespoon thinly sliced scallions, green parts only

I like to dress up my deviled eggs. Try to find farm-fresh eggs, which will have bright yellow yolks that make the filling stand out. You can easily prep these in advance and assemble them at the last minute. Use a piping bag to fill the whites with the yolks to make these look extra fancy.

Place the eggs in a medium saucepan and add cold water to cover by 2 inches. Bring to a boil, then reduce to a simmer and cook for 8 minutes. Remove the saucepan from the heat and cover; let the eggs sit for 10 minutes.

Drain off the hot water and place the eggs in a colander. Run cold water over the eggs until cool enough to handle. Carefully peel the eggs and rinse to remove any small bits of shell that might remain on the outside. Cut each egg in half and carefully scoop out the yolks.

Place the yolks in a medium mixing bowl and reserve the whites on a platter. To the yolks, add the aïoli, mustard, and vinegar; whisk vigorously until the lumps are mostly smoothed out and the yolks become creamy in texture. Season with salt and pepper.

Using a piping bag or a small spoon, fill the egg whites with the yolk mixture. Place a piece of salmon on top of each egg half. Divide the caviar, spooning a small amount over each of the eggs. Garnish with scallions.

New England Clam Chowder

SERVES 6 TO 8

18 cherrystone clams, well cleaned (see page 41)

3 cups clam juice

6 slices bacon

2 tablespoons unsalted butter

½ cup diced yellow onion

½ cup diced celery

¼ cup diced leek

⅓ cup unbleached all-purpose flour

3 cups half-and-half

2 bay leaves

2 cups diced (unpeeled) red potato

Kosher salt

2 teaspoons freshly squeezed lemon juice

2 teaspoons Worcestershire sauce

2 teaspoons Tabasco sauce

Freshly ground black pepper

1 tablespoon chopped flat-leaf parsley leaves

1 cup crumbled Saltines (page 221)

Chowder is as old as New England, and every cook I know has a favorite way of making it. It's a rich and filling soup by nature, but it shouldn't be too thick. My recipe is a slightly simplified version. If you want to make a classic chowder, replace the bacon with salt pork (being careful not to over-salt the soup at the end).

Place the clams in a Dutch oven with 2 cups of the clam juice. Cover and bring to a simmer over medium heat and cook until the clams open. Remove the clams with a slotted spoon and let cool slightly. Pick the meat from the shells and chop the meat into thirds; set aside. Strain the cooking liquid and reserve. Clean out the Dutch oven.

Line a plate with paper towels. Cut the bacon into ½-inch pieces and place in the Dutch oven. Cook over medium heat so that the bacon renders slowly. When the bacon is very crisp, use a slotted spoon to transfer it to the prepared plate, leaving the fat in the pan. Add the butter to the bacon fat and stir until melted.

Lower the heat to medium-low and add the onion, celery, and leek; sauté for 4 minutes. Add the flour a little at a time, stirring well with a wooden spoon or rubber spatula to combine between additions and scraping the bottom of the pan to make sure the mixture doesn't stick. When the flour is incorporated, add all of the reserved and remaining clam juice and stir to combine. Bring to a simmer while stirring constantly. Add the half-and-half. Return to a simmer, still stirring to ensure the soup does not burn on the bottom. Add the bay leaves and simmer over medium heat for 15 minutes, stirring occasionally.

While the chowder is simmering, put the diced potato in a medium saucepan and add cold water to cover. Season with salt, bring to a boil, then reduce the heat and simmer until tender, 10 to 12 minutes. Drain the potato and set aside.

To finish the chowder, remove and discard the bay leaves and stir in the clams, crispy bacon, potato, lemon juice, Worcestershire sauce, and Tabasco. Season with salt and pepper. Garnish each serving with chopped parsley and crumbled saltines.

Saison-Steamed Littlenecks with Parsley Butter and Grilled Sourdough

For this dish, I use a saison ale brewed by Trillium, an amazing brewery located just around the corner from Row 34 in Boston. Saison is a great flavor match with clams, but lager and pilsner work well, too. Place this dish in the center of the table and let everyone serve themselves. A note: If you have a stubborn clam that only opens slightly after cooking, carefully try to pry it open using a clam or butter knife.

In a large stockpot with a tight-fitting lid, heat the canola oil over medium heat. Add the shallot, garlic, and white parts of the scallions and sauté until they begin to color lightly, 2 to 3 minutes. Add the clams and the beer, cover, and let steam until the clams start to open, about 8 minutes.

As the clams open, use a slotted spoon to transfer them from the pot to a serving bowl. Repeat this until all the clams are open and in the serving bowl, leaving most of the cooking liquid in the pot. Add the lemon juice and parsley butter to the liquid and whisk until the butter melts. Taste the sauce—it should be salty. Season with salt and pepper as needed, then pour the sauce over the clams. Garnish with the scallion greens and serve sourdough on the side.

SERVES 4 AS AN APPETIZER

3 tablespoons canola oil

1 tablespoon minced shallot

1 teaspoon minced garlic

4 whole scallions, thinly sliced, white and green parts separated

40 littleneck clams, cleaned (see page 41)

1 cup saison, preferably Trillium Brewery's Saison Du Row

1 tablespoon freshly squeezed lemon juice

3 tablespoons Parsley Butter (see page 226)

Kosher salt and freshly ground black pepper

4 slices grilled or toasted sourdough bread

How to Shuck a Clam

A good clam shucking knife is an essential tool. Once you have one, shucking clams is easier than you expect.

Step 1. Hold a clam firmly in the palm of your hand with the hinge tucked into your palm. Place the edge of a clam shucking knife between the top and bottom shells.

Step 2. Using the fingers on the hand holding the clam, push the blade into the clam while using your other hand to push the handle in the same direction.

Step 3. When the knife is inside the clam, carefully scrape along the top shell to loosen the clam meat from the shell. Repeat with the bottom shell to leave the clam floating in the bottom shell. Serve on ice.

Fried Clams

This is as classic New England as it gets. As the story goes, fried clams were invented at Woodman's in Essex, Massachusetts, about 100 years ago. We use the same clams for frying as we do for steamers: I'm partial to using smaller clams for frying, since it takes less time to get them nice and crispy. You'll want to buy pre-shucked fry clams for this recipe; your fish counter might need a day or two advance notice. If you are not in New England, these are also available online. Before you get started, see Frying Seafood at Home on page 15.

Place the clams and buttermilk in a large bowl, stir to combine, then refrigerate for about 30 minutes.

Line a plate with paper towels. In a straight-sided skillet or Dutch oven, heat the canola oil to 350°F. Drain the clams, discarding the buttermilk. Place the seasoned flour in a clean bowl and add the clams, then toss well to coat. Make sure the individual clams are not sticking together. Fry the clams in the oil, working in batches if necessary, until crispy, 2 to 3 minutes.

Use a slotted spoon or skimmer to transfer the clams to the prepared plate to drain. Season with salt and pepper. Serve on a platter with lemon wedges and tartar sauce.

SERVES 4 AS A LIGHT APPETIZER

1 pound pre-shucked soft-shell clams

1 cup buttermilk

4 cups canola oil

3 cups Seasoned Flour (page 229)

Kosher salt and freshly ground black pepper

6 lemon wedges (see page 43)

1 cup Tartar Sauce (page 224)

Crispy Fish Sandwiches with Spicy Aïoli and Bread and Butter Pickles

SERVES 4 AS AN ENTRÉE

1 pound pollock filet, cut into 4 pieces

½ cup buttermilk

1 cup canola oil

1 cup Seasoned Flour (page 229)

Kosher salt and freshly ground black pepper

4 brioche buns

6 large romaine lettuce leaves, thinly sliced

⅓ cup Spicy Aïoli (page 225)

½ cup Bread and Butter Pickles (page 214)

2 cups Coleslaw (page 210)

1 batch Potato Chips (page 216)

Never underestimate how delicious a really good fish sandwich can be. I almost always use pollock for this crispy sandwich since it's a sturdy fish, but a lot of different species will work in its place. I generally use the tail ends of whole filets, as those pieces are about the same size as a brioche bun. You can also substitute grilled salmon for a great variation on this sandwich but if you're following the recipe, see Frying Seafood at Home on page 15.

Place the pollock in a large bowl, pour the buttermilk over the pollock, and allow to soak for a few minutes.

Meanwhile, line a plate with paper towels. Place the oil in a straight-sided skillet that's large enough to hold two of the pieces of fish at a time and heat the oil over medium-high heat.

Place the seasoned flour in a large shallow dish. Remove the fish from the buttermilk, discarding the liquid, and add the fish to the seasoned flour, turning to coat each piece well. Once the oil is hot, fry 2 of the pieces of fish, turning once, until crispy and golden brown on both sides. Remove with a slotted spatula, transfer to the prepared plate to drain, and repeat with the remaining 2 pieces. Season with salt and pepper.

Lightly toast the buns. In a medium bowl, toss together the sliced romaine and the aïoli. Chop the pickles and fold into the lettuce mixture. To assemble, place one filet on the bottom portion of each bun and top with some of the romaine and pickle mixture. Top with the other halves of the buns and serve with coleslaw and potato chips.

Crispy Fish Tacos with Vegetable Slaw and Lime Crema

These tacos are easy and versatile. You can replace the fried fish with fried oysters or grilled fish—they'll still turn out great. If you don't have everything on hand to make the tempura batter, you can use a little buttermilk and seasoned flour to coat the fish instead. Pollock is ideal for this dish but most whitefish, and even shrimp, work well in its place. Make the slaw an hour or so in advance to give the vegetables time to marinate.

Line a plate with paper towels. In a straight-sided skillet or Dutch oven, heat the canola oil to 350° F.

Meanwhile, pat the pollock pieces dry with a paper towel and place them in a large shallow dish. Pour the tempura batter over the fish, then turn each piece of fish to coat.

To fry, dip half of a piece of fish in the oil while holding the other half out of the oil for 10 seconds. Carefully let go of the piece so it slides into the oil. This will prevent the fish from sticking to the bottom. Repeat with each piece of fish, working in batches if necessary to keep from crowding the pan. Fry until crisp, 3 to 5 minutes, lowering the heat slightly if the batter seems to be browning very quickly.

Using a slotted spoon or skimmer, carefully transfer the pieces of fish to the prepared plate to drain as they are fried. Season with salt and pepper. Repeat with remaining fish, ensuring that the oil is back up to temperature before you fry the next round. Reserve the oil.

Transfer about 1 teaspoon of the frying oil to a clean skillet and place over medium heat. Place a tortilla in the pan and toast for 15 seconds on each side. Transfer to a serving platter and repeat with remaining tortillas, arranging them in a single layer

MAKES 12 TACOS

4 cups canola oil

12 ounces pollock filet, cut into 12 pieces

2 cups Tempura Batter (page 229)

Kosher salt and freshly ground black pepper

Twelve 6-inch corn tortillas

1 cup Vegetable Slaw (following page)

½ cup Lime Crema (following page)

4 scallions, green parts only, thinly sliced

2 tablespoons roughly chopped cilantro

MAKES ABOUT 1 CUP

1 tablespoon grated ginger

¼ cup rice wine vinegar

1 tablespoon honey

1 tablespoon sriracha hot sauce

2 teaspoons sesame oil

1 cup sliced Napa cabbage

¼ cup sliced red onion

¼ cup sliced red bell pepper

1 small jalapeño, seeded and
thinly sliced

Kosher salt and freshly ground
black pepper

FOR THE LIME CREMA

MAKES ABOUT ½ CUP

¼ cup sour cream

¼ cup crème fraîche

Finely grated zest of 1 lime

3 tablespoons freshly squeezed
lime juice

Kosher salt and freshly ground
black pepper

on the serving platter. Spoon a little of the slaw into the center of each tortilla and place a piece of fish on top of each mound of slaw. Drizzle the crema over the fish and garnish with the scallion greens and cilantro.

Vegetable Slaw

In a medium bowl, whisk together the ginger, vinegar, honey, sriracha, and sesame oil. Add the cabbage, red onion, bell pepper, and jalapeño to the bowl. Toss a few times to coat the vegetables. Season with salt and pepper. Refrigerate until ready to use.

Lime Crema

In a small bowl, combine the sour cream, crème fraîche, lime zest, and juice. Season with salt and pepper. Refrigerate until ready to use.

Creamy White Grits with Brown Butter Lobster Knuckles

My coauthor on this book, Erin Byers Murray, wrote the book on grits. (Check out *Grits: A Cultural and Culinary Journey Through the South*.) This dish brings together two things that we both love: grits and lobster. Both ingredients have humble origins but are now celebrated on tables around the country. Paired together, they make a simple-to-prepare yet decadent dish that's become a Row 34 favorite all year long.

In a medium saucepan, combine the stock and milk. Bring to a boil and season with salt and pepper. Add the grits in a thin stream while whisking constantly. When all of the grits have been added, lower the heat to medium-low; the grits should be just barely bubbling. Stir frequently, keeping a close watch on the saucepan, as the grits like to burn on the bottom. Cook the grits until smooth and creamy and no longer raw tasting, about 1 hour and 20 minutes. If they become too thick during the cooking process, add a little more vegetable stock and stir well. Whisk in 2 tablespoons butter and the crème fraîche. Keep warm.

In a large sauté pan, heat the remaining 6 tablespoons butter over medium heat until it just begins to brown lightly. Add the shallot and sauté for 10 seconds. Add the lobster knuckles and brown very lightly in the butter until just heated through. Remove the pan from the heat, stir in the lemon juice, and season with salt and pepper.

Divide the grits among four individual bowls. Make a small well in the center of the grits. Divide the lobster knuckles into four portions, spooning the meat and butter sauce over the grits. Garnish with the parsley and serve warm.

SERVES 4 AS AN APPETIZER

1½ cups Vegetable Stock (page 230)

1 cup whole milk

Kosher salt and freshly ground black pepper

½ cup (uncooked) white grits

1 stick (8 tablespoons) unsalted butter

2 tablespoons crème fraîche

1 shallot, minced

1 cup cooked lobster knuckles, removed from shell (see page 124)

1 teaspoon freshly squeezed lemon juice

1 tablespoon chopped flat-leaf parsley leaves

Grilled Lobsters with Drawn Butter

SERVES 4 AS AN ENTRÉE

4 sticks (1 pound) unsalted butter

4 sprigs thyme

Kosher salt

4 lobsters, 1¼ to 1½ pounds each

8 lemon wedges (see page 43)

1 batch Roasted Potatoes
(page 208)

1 batch Grilled Corn Salad
(page 211)

Giving lobsters a quick boil to set the meat in the shell, then finishing them on the grill is one of my favorite ways to eat lobster in the summertime. The lobsters can be partially cooked and cleaned a day ahead. For this preparation, I much prefer wood or charcoal over gas, but any grill will do. Pay a little extra attention to the claws, especially if they're large. You can always remove the claws from the body and grill them a little longer if they're not quite finished cooking.

Light a wood or charcoal grill, or heat a gas grill to medium-high.

In a medium saucepan, combine the butter and thyme and heat until the butter is melted. Remove and discard the thyme sprigs.

In a large stockpot, bring 2 gallons of salted water to a boil. Drop the lobsters into the water and cook for 6 minutes. Remove the lobsters and set aside until cool enough to handle.

With a large knife, carefully split the lobsters down the middle and crack the claws just enough to expose the meat. Remove the innards of the lobsters. Place each lobster half on the hot grill, shell-side down. As the lobsters cook, spin the pieces around, keeping them shell-side down, so that each piece cooks evenly. When the tail meat looks firm and cooked through, flip the lobsters over so that they're meat-side down on the grill and cook for 1 additional minute.

Transfer the lobsters from the grill to a serving platter. Brush the meat with some of the thyme butter. Serve the lobsters with remaining butter and lemon wedges on the side, along with the potatoes and corn salad.

How to Clean and Cook Lobsters

Buying and cooking lobsters should be an event. Not only are they really cool, but they're absolutely one of the best tasting shellfish, hands down. As with all food, the closer you are to the source the better it tastes—but living in a landlocked state shouldn't preclude you from buying lobster once in a while, especially since you can mail order from places all over the country. Look for live lobsters—they should be active and annoyed when you pick them up. If they're limp and don't move much they've probably been out of the water for some time. Lobsters that sit in tanks for long periods of time never taste as good. One marker of a good lobster is long antennae, a sign that your chosen lobster probably hasn't been in the tank for long. (Crowded, hungry lobsters tend to eat each other's antennae.)

What You Need

Wherever you get your lobsters, plan on cooking them the same day. It takes a little bit of work to cook and clean them, so make sure you're all set up in advance. You'll need a large stockpot (big enough to hold at least 2 lobsters at a time), a cocktail fork, lobster crackers or a heavy French knife, and a large vessel filled with ice to cool them in (you can also use a sink filled with lots of ice) if you're not eating the lobster right away.

How to Cook Them

At Row 34, we cook thousands of pounds of lobster each week. We've developed a few methods to make the process as efficient as possible. For one, we usually remove the tails and claws from the lobsters before cooking them. You can do this by holding a towel around a lobster and twisting the tail from the body; do the same with the claws. Raw bodies, after they've been cleaned, are better for stocks than cooked ones, but really both will work. If you don't feel like ripping apart a live lobster (understandable!), cooking them whole works as well.

Fill your large stockpot about ¾ full with water, measuring the water as you go. Add ¼ cup of salt per gallon of water. Bring the water to a rapid boil and add the lobsters. Cover the pot.

A 1¼-pound lobster cooks in 11 minutes. Add 3 minutes of cooking time for every ¼ pound you go up in size. Once the lobsters are red and firm to the touch, remove them from the water and plunge them into the bowl of ice water.

How to Clean Them

Once a lobster is cool enough to handle, remove the tail and claws from the bodies. The knuckle is the piece that is connected to the claw; remove the knuckle by holding the claw and pressing it against a table to snap it away from the claw. Use a cocktail fork to remove the pieces of meat from both ends of the knuckle.

For the claws you can use a lobster cracker or a French knife. Carefully remove the movable "thumb" of the claw and the attached piece of cartilage from the center of the claw; some meat should come with it. Using the cracker or the handle end of the blade, carefully crack one side of the claw at the end where the knuckle was attached. Flip the claw and repeat. The two cracks should connect, and the base of the shell should fall off exposing the claw meat. Gently pull the meat from the shell.

There are two ways to approach the tail. The first is to lay the tail flat on a cutting board and with a

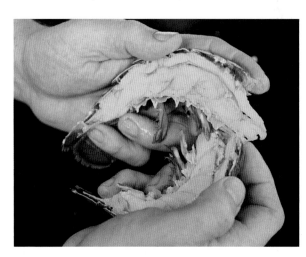

French knife cut through the center of the shell lengthwise, exposing the tail meat. Remove the meat from the two sides of the tail. If the lobster is really hard-shelled or too big to cut with a knife, you can use lobster crackers: Starting at the tail end, crack the shell in three or four spots until you can pull the shell apart by hand.

Lobster meat can be refrigerated in an airtight container for up to 3 days.

Warm Buttered Lobster Rolls

This is easily one of the all-time most popular dishes at Row 34. People always ask me if I prefer this one or the classic lobster roll, but I truly don't have a favorite. If you hand me either roll, I'm going to eat it! This warm buttered version is associated with Connecticut, while the classic, creamy lobster salad has its roots in Maine. Don't discard the butter after warming the lobster. Refrigerate it to use again later, or make a butter sauce with it.

Brush the sides of the buns with some of the melted butter. In a sauté pan that's large enough to hold all of the lobster meat, toast the buns lightly over medium heat for a few minutes on each side. Remove the buns and set aside.

Add the rest of the melted butter to the pan and heat over medium heat until it reaches 180° F; the butter should be bubbling lightly but not boiling. The goal is to get hot melted butter that doesn't brown. Add the lobster meat to the pan and stir to coat the lobster pieces completely in butter. Stir in the salt. Cook until the lobster is sizzling again, then remove the pan from the heat and let the lobster sit in the pan until warmed through, about 3 minutes.

Use a slotted spoon to remove the lobster from the butter, letting the excess butter drip off. Fill each toasted hot dog bun with lobster meat. Serve with coleslaw and potato chips.

SERVES 4 AS AN ENTRÉE

4 top-loaded hot dog buns

1½ sticks (12 tablespoons) unsalted butter, melted

1 pound cooked lobster meat, chopped into 2-inch pieces (see page 124)

2 teaspoons sea salt

2 cups Coleslaw (page 210)

1 batch Potato Chips (page 216)

top: Warm Buttered Lobster Rolls, this page
bottom: Ethel's Classic Lobster Rolls, page 128

Ethel's Classic Lobster Rolls

SERVES 4 AS AN ENTRÉE

1 pound cooked lobster meat, chopped into 2-inch pieces (see page 124)

3 tablespoons minced celery

3 tablespoons minced dill pickle

2 tablespoons minced red onion

2 teaspoons freshly squeezed lemon juice

½ teaspoon celery salt, plus more for garnish (optional)

½ cup Mayonnaise (page 224)

3 tablespoons crème fraîche

Kosher salt and freshly ground black pepper

4 tablespoons unsalted butter

4 top-loaded hot dog rolls

2 cups Coleslaw (page 210)

1 batch Potato Chips (page 216)

Ethel was my grandmother and the wife of a lobsterman. By the time I came around, my grandfather only ate hot dogs at family lobster cookouts because he'd gotten his fill of lobster when it was the only thing they had to eat. The day after a family cookout, we would pick out all the leftover lobster meat and make lobster rolls for a special treat. What I think makes this lobster roll unique is my grandmother's addition of dill pickles, which contribute snap. Go easy on the salt in the salad, especially if you're opting to use the celery salt at the end.

In a large bowl, combine the lobster meat with the celery, pickle, red onion, lemon juice, ½ teaspoon celery salt, mayonnaise, and crème fraîche. Season with salt and pepper.

In a large skillet, melt the butter and toast the hot dog rolls in the butter on both sides. Divide the lobster salad among the rolls and sprinkle each roll with a little celery salt, if desired. Serve with coleslaw and chips.

Oyster Burgers with Togarashi Aïoli

It's a bit of work to get all the different components for this burger together, but believe me, it's worth the effort. The onions, bacon, and aïoli can all be made in advance—just make sure to warm the onions and bacon before assembling. If your patties are thin or small, decrease the cooking time. And definitely serve these with 242 Fries (page 218).

Preheat the oven to 425° F.

Line a plate with paper towels. Arrange the bacon in a single layer on a baking sheet and bake until crisp, 18 to 20 minutes. Transfer to the prepared plate to drain; pour any remaining bacon fat from the pan into a glass jar or bowl and set aside.

Line another plate with paper towels. Heat the canola oil in a sauté pan over medium heat and add the sliced onions. Cook, stirring frequently, until the onions begin to color. When the onions are just starting to darken, add the reserved bacon fat and lower the heat.

Continue cooking over medium-low heat until the onions begin to take on a caramel color, stirring often so that they don't stick to the pan. Season with salt and pepper. Transfer the onions from the pan to the prepared plate to drain off excess fat.

Preheat a grill to medium-high heat.

Brush each burger patty with a little of the butter and season liberally with salt and pepper. Place the burgers on the hot grill and cook for 2 minutes. Rotate the burgers, keeping the same side down. Repeat this one more time, cooking the burgers for 6 minutes on that side. Flip the burger and cook for an additional 3 to 4 minutes. Remove the burgers from the grill and let rest for 2 to 3 minutes.

MAKES 4 BURGERS

8 slices bacon

2 tablespoons canola oil

2 yellow onions, thinly sliced

Kosher salt and freshly ground
    black pepper

2 pounds ground beef, formed
    into 4 patties

3 tablespoons unsalted butter, at
    room temperature

4 brioche buns, halved

¼ cup Togarashi Aïoli (page 225)

8 fried oysters (see page 35)

While the burgers are resting, brush the remaining butter over the cut sides of each brioche bun and toast on the grill, cut sides down, for about 3 minutes.

To assemble, place the grilled burgers on the bottom buns. Top each burger with 2 slices bacon, a spoonful of sautéed onions, a dollop of aïoli, and 2 fried oysters. Place the other halves of the buns on top and press down lightly to hold everything together. Spear two long toothpicks into each burger on opposite sides, then cut the burgers in half so that the toothpicks keep each half intact. Serve hot.

Beer-Battered Fish and Chips with Malt Vinegar Aïoli

A solid plate of fish and chips should be crispy, flaky, and not in any way greasy. Pollock, cod, hake, and haddock are all good choices. Try to get four pieces of fish that are about the same thickness; I like using tail pieces. Or, for something different, you can batter and fry shrimp or scallops to serve with the chips. Instead of splashing malt vinegar on top of crispy fish, I like dipping my fish in malt vinegar aïoli—it's great with fries, too. Fry the 242 Fries first, then hold them in a warm oven while you cook the fish.

Line a plate with paper towels. In a Dutch oven, heat the oil to 350°F.

Use a paper towel to thoroughly pat dry each piece of fish, then place the fish pieces in the batter, coating all sides well. Using tongs, carefully place a piece of fish in the frying oil by holding one corner of the piece until it's three-quarters submerged. Count to 10, then let the entire piece drop down into the oil. (This will prevent the fish from sticking to the bottom of the pan.) Repeat this process with each piece of fish. Fry for 2 minutes, then flip the fish over and fry for another 2 minutes. The fish should be golden brown on both sides; do this in batches if necessary.

Remove the fish from the frying oil and transfer to the prepared plate to drain. Season with salt and pepper. Serve with lemon wedges, fries, and aïoli for dipping.

Beer Batter

In a large bowl, mix together all of the dry ingredients. Whisk in the beer and soda water until smooth. Refrigerate until ready to use.

SERVES 4 AS AN ENTRÉE

4 cups canola oil

2 cups Beer Batter (below)

1½ pounds pollock or other white fish, cut into 4 pieces

Kosher salt and freshly ground black pepper

1 lemon, cut into wedges (see page 43)

1 batch 242 Fries (page 218)

1 cup Malt Vinegar Aïoli (page 224)

FOR THE BEER BATTER

MAKES ABOUT 2 CUPS

¾ cup unbleached all-purpose flour

¼ cup rice flour

1 tablespoon kosher salt

1 teaspoon baking soda

1 teaspoon baking powder

6 ounces beer

3 ounces soda or sparkling water

Spicy Fish Soup

3 tablespoons canola oil

½ cup diced carrot

½ cup diced red onion

½ cup diced sweet potato

¼ cup diced red bell pepper

¼ cup sliced celery

2 teaspoons grated ginger

1 teaspoon grated garlic

1 tablespoon red curry paste

1½ cups Fish Stock (page 230)

8 ounces mixed fish (see headnote)

1 cup coconut milk

1 cup cooked brown rice

Kosher salt and freshly ground black pepper

2 teaspoons sesame oil

1 small jalapeño, seeded and sliced into thin rounds (optional)

3 large mint leaves

6 large basil leaves

½ lime

Any time you have little pieces of fish and seafood left over, wrap them well and freeze them: frozen is better than wasted. You can use those pieces, or any fish, in this spicy soup. Pieces of lobster, shrimp, monkfish, halibut, and salmon are some of my favorites. This soup is inspired by a combination of Asian flavors and is a variation of a soup we frequently make for our staff meal. We've gotten pretty good at making it, so now, spicy fish soup occasionally finds its way onto the menu. Add or remove vegetables as you like—this is meant to be flavorful and rustic. I prefer to eat this with crusty bread to dip into the broth.

In a large pot or Dutch oven, heat the canola oil over medium heat. Add the carrot, onion, sweet potato, bell pepper, and celery and sauté until they begin to soften. Stir in the ginger and garlic and cook for 30 seconds. Stir in the red curry paste and combine until everything is coated.

Add the stock and bring to a simmer. Let simmer until the vegetables are almost fully cooked, about 5 minutes. Add the fish pieces, return to a simmer, and cook until the fish is cooked through, about 3 minutes. Stir in the coconut milk and brown rice. Season with salt and pepper.

Just before serving, add the sesame oil and jalapeño slices, if using. Tear the mint and basil leaves and stir into the soup. Squeeze some lime juice over the top of each serving.

Mussels Steamed in White Wine and Garlic Broth

Like so many shellfish dishes, this one is a great communal meal that should be eaten with your hands to fully enjoy it. Almost all the mussels you find these days are farmed—which means they're widely available year-round, and they're inexpensive. This recipe is great because everything comes together in about 10 minutes. Leave the thyme and bay leaf in the liquid when you serve—you can pick around them. And if there are any uneaten mussels left over, use them in another dish—they're great tossed with garlic and butter and served over linguine.

In a large sauté pan with a lid, heat the canola oil over medium heat. Add the garlic and shallot and sweat until they begin to color lightly, 2 to 3 minutes. Add the mussels, white wine, bay leaf, and thyme and cover. Steam the mussels until they begin to open, 3 to 4 minutes.

Use a slotted spoon to transfer the mussels to a serving bowl, leaving most of the liquid in the pan. Bring the liquid to a boil and whisk in the butter and Dijon mustard until the butter has melted. Season with salt and pepper. Pour the liquid over the mussels. Garnish with parsley and serve with sourdough bread.

SERVES 4 AS AN APPETIZER

3 tablespoons canola oil

2 tablespoons minced garlic

2 tablespoons minced shallot

3 pounds mussels, cleaned and beards removed (see page 41)

1½ cups dry white wine

1 bay leaf

3 sprigs thyme

1 stick (8 tablespoons) unsalted butter, cut into chunks

2 teaspoons Dijon mustard

Kosher salt and freshly ground black pepper

2 tablespoons roughly chopped flat-leaf parsley leaves

4 slices grilled sourdough bread

How Fishing Changed My Life

by Ryan Boyd, Chef de Cuisine, Row 34 Portsmouth

I love to fish. It's become my main outlet for connecting to the food I cook—but it's also grown into so much more for me. Fishing has taught me how much work and skill goes into catching the wild fish that we serve in our restaurants, as well as to appreciate the beauty of the natural world. But my life has not always been filled with catching massive striped bass off the Chatham coast or fishing for North Atlantic cod in Norway. I was put on this path when I met Jeremy Sewall while I was in culinary school and applying to become an extern at his Brookline restaurant Lineage.

Starting my career at Lineage was the best thing that could have happened to me. Working at Lineage taught me everything from setting up my station to classic cooking techniques. And, most importantly, it was at Lineage that I learned how to butcher and cook fish. Lineage was well-known for using local dayboat fish, and a position working the fish station had to be earned. When I was a nineteen-year-old extern it became my only goal. That marked the beginning of my respect for everything related to fish and drove my need to understand more about how the fish got to us and then to guests. While there, I learned about fish that I'd never heard of before, from monkfish, hake, and tilefish to the coveted striped bass.

All of this was tied together with the lobster we were sourcing from Jeremy's cousin Mark out of York, Maine, and our weekly trips to the Brookline farmer's market. Each week, the entire staff would walk over to the market with a cart and fill it to the brim with local veggies from the Boston area. We competed to see who could find the best deals or the ingredients for specials that would sell the best each night. It was all so eye-opening.

We created our menus every single day and doing so enabled us to adjust easily based on what the fishermen and farmers were bringing to market. This constant flow of the menu was an education in itself; I had to keep up with the changes and learn how to use new products from day to day. Meanwhile, the product chain was starting to form in my head—I was seeing where our products were from and how local fish were delivered to our back door each day. But nothing was more important in connecting the dots for me than when Jeremy took the Lineage crew striped bass fishing for the first time on Cape Cod.

I had never been fishing in the ocean before. My first trip was with Captain Darren Saletta out of Ryder's Cove in Chatham. It was a life-changing experience to say the least. I'd fished in some local ponds as a kid growing up in central Massachusetts, but nothing compared to hooking a thirty-pound striped bass with light tackle gear and hearing my reel scream as the line was being taken out by the speeding fish. The fish was as majestic as it was strong. After I caught that first one, I was hooked myself—on the rush of adrenaline.

Once we made a catch, I paid attention to the care that Darren put into killing the fish the proper way: cutting the throat so it bled out quickly, making sure that all of the blood drained from the body, and thoroughly icing it down to preserve the meat. He took many steps to ensure that none of the fish would be wasted. That's how much respect he has for these animals. I've kept that same mentality ever since. Until then, I'd had plenty of striped bass on my cutting board without ever seeing them as once-living creatures. But I've tried to use every part of every fish I've cut since that first fishing trip, including preparing the filets, making ceviche with the trim, and cooking stock with the bodies.

Along the way, I've learned much about the hard work that goes into getting high-quality products into our restaurants. You can see the work everyone puts into their products, from the hard-working fishermen and women bringing in their daily catches, to the farmers growing heirloom squash, to the oyster farmers who deliver their harvests. You can see it in the food itself and on these people's clothes, their hands, and their faces. Every one of them is damn proud to sell us their products.

I've been fortunate to fish with Darren many times over the years, and when my then-girlfriend Ally

(who is now the chef de cuisine at Row 34 Boston) started to work for Jeremy, she earned her spot on the fishing trips as well. She quickly fell in love with all that goes into harvesting wild fish and the act of fishing. Ally and I have since gotten married and fishing is something we do together year-round.

Since we caught our first striped bass with Jeremy and Darren, fishing has become a passion that drives our professional and personal lives. It has become a tool for education for both of us within the restaurants. Becoming a good fisherman means understanding your "prey." How fish swim, what they eat, and where they live in the water all relates to how they taste and how they should be cooked. Fishing was a way to better

my skills within the kitchen. And, on the personal side, fishing has become a place of refuge—Ally and I escape to the water and unwind from work. On our days off you can usually find us surf casting for striped bass during the summer or fly-fishing for trout in a mountain stream during the fall. Fishing even filled our honeymoon: We spent our days fly-fishing the flats of Belize for bonefish and barracuda.

Throughout the years of fishing with Jeremy I have learned two major things. Fishing can be a way to relax and get into nature. But more importantly, fishing can be a way to complete the circle of understanding about where the food on your plate is coming from and the dedication and skill it takes to get it there.

CHAPTER FOUR

The Whole Fish

Salt Cod Croquettes with Tomato Aïoli

Salt cod helped shape the modern world. Cod was one of the most abundant species on the planet at one point, with people traveling from all over the world to harvest cod off the New England coast. Before refrigeration, after cod was caught it was salted and packed into barrels to travel across the ocean. Making salt cod can be a little time consuming but it's easy—and it's a great way to use up the trimmings of a whole fish. If you are salting small pieces, cut down on the time they sit under the salt. For frying tips, see Frying Seafood at Home (page 15), and be sure to taste the croquettes once they've been fried before you add any final seasoning—they might not need much salt at all.

In a medium sauté pan, heat the canola oil over medium heat. Add the onion and garlic and sauté until soft, but don't let the mixture color. Remove from heat and let cool to room temperature.

Preheat the oven to 350°F.

Fill a medium saucepan with cold, salted water. Add the potato pieces and bring to a simmer. Cook until tender, 8 to 10 minutes. Drain well and place on a baking sheet; let dry in the oven for 5 minutes, then let cool slightly.

Place the potato in a large bowl and mash it with a fork. Add the sautéed onions and garlic, egg yolks, paprika, lemon zest, and parsley. Mix all ingredients together and then fold in the salt cod, breaking it up with the fork as you do. Continue mixing until incorporated.

Using a small ice cream scoop or spoon, divide the salt cod mixture into balls about 1½ inches in diameter, rolling them with your hands to round them. Fill three soup bowls, one with the

SERVES 4 AS AN APPETIZER

1 tablespoon canola oil

½ cup minced yellow onion

1 teaspoon minced garlic

1 large russet potato, peeled and cut into 2-inch pieces

2 egg yolks

¼ teaspoon smoked paprika

1 teaspoon finely grated lemon zest

1 tablespoon chopped flat-leaf parsley leaves

1 filet Salt Cod (following page)

½ cup unbleached all-purpose flour

2 large eggs, beaten

1 cup breadcrumbs

Vegetable oil for frying

Kosher salt and freshly ground black pepper

½ cup Tomato Aïoli (page 224)

1 cup kosher salt

1 cod filet, about 8 ounces

2 cups whole milk

flour, one with the eggs, and one with the breadcrumbs. Dredge a ball in flour, dip it in the egg, and dredge it in the breadcrumbs to coat all sides. Repeat with the remaining balls, setting them aside in a single layer on a large plate or platter.

Line a plate with paper towels. Fill a large straight-sided skillet or Dutch oven with several inches of vegetable oil—enough to submerge the croquettes. Heat the frying oil to 350°F. Fry the croquettes, in batches to keep from crowding the pan, until golden brown and crisp. Use a slotted spoon to transfer them to the prepared plate as they are cooked. Once the croquettes are cool enough to handle, taste one for salt. Season with salt and pepper and serve hot with Tomato Aïoli on the side for dipping.

Salt Cod

Place ⅓ of the salt in the bottom of a shallow dish and lay the cod flat on top of the salt. Cover the cod with the remaining salt and refrigerate for 24 hours. Remove the cod filet and rinse off the salt under running water. Place the filet in a medium bowl and add water to cover. Soak the cod in the refrigerator for 6 hours, changing the water twice during that time.

Remove the cod from the water, place the filet in a small saucepan, and add the milk. Over medium heat, bring the milk to a simmer. Remove from the heat and let the cod sit for 10 minutes in the warm milk. Drain and discard the liquid.

Grilled Salmon Collars with Cucumber Salad and Tzatziki Sauce

Fish collars have incredible tasty bits of meat on them, but they're not always available, so call your fishmonger in advance to request the collars. Ask to have the scales removed from the skin-sides of the collars and request that they be trimmed of any excess skin. The heat from the harissa and the coolness of the cucumbers enhances the strong flavor. I like these hot off the grill, but they can also be done in a hot oven, around 400° F. If salmon collars aren't available, this method works with almost any type of fish collar.

In a large bowl, whisk together the lemon juice, harissa, garlic, and olive oil. Add the salmon collars to the bowl and turn them several times to be sure they're fully coated. Refrigerate for at least 1 hour and up to 3 hours.

Heat a grill to high heat.

Remove the collars from the marinade; let excess marinade drain off. Place the collars skin-side down on the hot grill. Move them frequently to prevent flare ups. Cook the collars all the way through, 6 to 8 minutes.

Pile the salad in the center of a serving plate or platter. Place the grilled collars on top. Serve the tzatziki on the side for dipping.

Cucumber Salad

In a medium bowl, combine the cucumber with the red onion, mint, lemon juice, and olive oil. Season with salt and pepper and refrigerate until ready to use.

SERVES 2 AS AN APPETIZER

1 tablespoon freshly squeezed lemon juice

1 teaspoon harissa

1 garlic clove, crushed

3 tablespoons extra-virgin olive oil

4 salmon collars

1 cup Cucumber Salad (below)

¾ cup Tzatziki Sauce (following page)

FOR THE CUCUMBER SALAD

MAKES ABOUT 1 CUP

1 cup peeled, halved, seeded, and sliced English cucumber

¼ cup very thinly sliced red onion

4 mint leaves, julienned

2 teaspoons freshly squeezed lemon juice

1 tablespoon extra-virgin olive oil

Kosher salt and freshly ground black pepper

2 tablespoons grated English cucumber

Kosher salt

¼ cup Greek yogurt

2 tablespoons sour cream

1 teaspoon minced garlic

1 tablespoon freshly squeezed lime juice

½ teaspoon chopped dill

Freshly ground black pepper

1 tablespoon extra-virgin olive oil

Tzatziki Sauce

In a small bowl, toss the grated cucumber with a few pinches of salt, then pour into a strainer to let drain. Press down on the cucumber with a paper towel to remove excess liquid.

In a medium bowl, stir together the cucumber, yogurt, sour cream, garlic, lime juice, and dill. Season with salt and pepper and refrigerate until ready to use. Once you're ready to serve, place the tzatziki sauce in a serving bowl for dipping and drizzle olive oil over the top.

Crispy Cod Cheeks with Crushed Peas and Lemon Aïoli

SERVES 4 AS AN APPETIZER

1 pound cod cheeks

½ cup buttermilk

2 teaspoons Tabasco sauce

2 tablespoons extra-virgin olive oil

1 tablespoon minced garlic

½ teaspoon curry powder

2 cups shelled English peas

¼ cup crème fraîche

Kosher salt and freshly ground black pepper

4 cups canola oil

2 cups Seasoned Flour (page 229)

¼ cup Lemon Aïoli (page 225)

Ask your local fish market to save fish cheeks for you when they're cutting fish. The cheeks on larger fish are little treasures that are worth seeking out. If you can't get cod cheeks, you can use the cheeks of halibut, monkfish, or almost any other fish for this recipe. I like to fry these using a method I use for a lot of seafood: dredged in seasoned flour and fried in canola oil. For more on frying, see Frying Seafood at Home (page 15). It's simple and tasty and allows the flavor to shine through. The recipe calls for a good amount of garlic, which I like, but feel free to use less.

In a medium bowl, combine the cod cheeks with the buttermilk and Tabasco and refrigerate for about 30 minutes.

Meanwhile, in a medium skillet over medium heat, heat the olive oil, then add the garlic and sauté until it begins to color slightly, 1 to 2 minutes. Remove from the heat and stir in the curry powder. Allow to cool.

Prepare an ice water bath. Bring a medium saucepan of salted water to a boil. Add the peas and blanch for 60 seconds. Dunk them in the ice water bath to stop the cooking. Drain the peas once cool, then combine them with the garlic-curry oil in the bowl of a food processor fitted with the metal blade and puree until the peas are crushed, about 15 seconds. Add the crème fraîche and puree for another 10 seconds. You don't want to overmix the peas once the crème fraîche has been added. Season with salt and pepper to taste. Set aside.

Line a plate with paper towels. Heat the canola oil in a large, straight-sided skillet or Dutch oven until it reaches 350°F.

Drain the cod cheeks from the buttermilk mixture. In a large bowl, toss the cheeks in the flour until the cheeks are well coated. Working in batches if necessary to keep from crowding the pan, fry the cheeks in the oil, turning them frequently, until crisp on all sides, about 2 minutes. Use a slotted spoon to move the cheeks to the prepared plate to drain.

To serve, warm the pea mixture in a small saucepan over medium heat. Spoon the crushed peas onto four plates and top each portion with a few crispy cod cheeks. Add a small dollop of aïoli on top of each serving.

Crispy Black Bass Collars with Ginger Sauce and Scallions

In case I haven't said it enough: make friends with your fish-mongers. Once you've established a rapport, you can make specific requests, such as setting aside the collars of fish for you as they're butchering. Black bass has become much more common up and down the East Coast—it's also one of my favorite fish to eat. Ask your fishmonger in advance for black bass collars specifically, but the collars of almost any fish of a similar size will work; grouper, snapper, and yellowtail collars are all good substitutes. This dish requires a little bit of time and effort, but it makes a very tasty snack or starter.

In a small bowl, whisk together the grated garlic and ginger with the soy sauce, sesame oil, lime juice, and sriracha. Refrigerate until ready to use.

Line a plate with paper towels. Fill a straight-sided skillet or Dutch oven with several inches of oil—enough to submerge the collars. Heat the oil to 350°F.

Meanwhile, in a large bowl, combine the rice flour with the sesame seeds and season with salt and pepper. In another large bowl, whisk together the egg white and 1 tablespoon water. Dredge a bass collar in the egg mixture. Remove, letting the excess egg white drip off the collar, then transfer it to the bowl with the rice flour. Repeat until all of the collars are in the rice flour. Coat each collar well with the flour and shake off any excess, then add to the oil and fry until crisp, 3 to 4 minutes, working in batches if necessary. Transfer the collars to the prepared plate to drain as they are finished. To serve, place the collars on a medium platter. Garnish with the scallion slices and serve the ginger sauce on the side for dipping.

SERVES 2 AS AN APPETIZER

1 garlic clove, grated

1 teaspoon grated ginger

½ cup soy sauce

1 teaspoon sesame oil

1 tablespoon freshly squeezed
   lime juice

1 teaspoon sriracha hot sauce

Canola oil for frying

1 cup rice flour

1 teaspoon white sesame seeds

Kosher salt and freshly ground
   black pepper

1 egg white

10 black bass collars

1 bunch scallions, green parts
   only, thinly sliced

Roasted Fish Heads

SERVES 2 TO 4 AS AN APPETIZER

¼ cup canola oil

2 tablespoons chopped shallot

1 tablespoon chopped garlic

2 fish heads, gills and scales
   removed

Kosher salt and freshly ground
   black pepper

2 tablespoons soy sauce

1 tablespoon honey

1 tablespoon rice wine vinegar

2 tablespoons freshly squeezed
   orange juice

1 teaspoon sriracha hot sauce

I know what you're thinking: Why would I eat a fish head? Well, not only is there a lot of meat on a fish head that shouldn't go to waste, but fish heads are also delicious. I like medium-size heads that weigh about 1½ pounds each. Call your fishmonger to request striper, larger black bass, snapper, or even salmon heads, which will all work in this recipe. Have them leave the collars on the heads, which will help them stand up; it will also ensure there's plenty of meat to pick at. (Most of the meat is on the top of the head and in the cheeks and the collar.) Invite your guests to use their hands to pull the fish heads apart—it makes for a really fun experience. Note: You might need to adjust the cooking time depending on the size of the heads.

Preheat the oven to 400° F.

In a small bowl, whisk together the canola oil, shallot, and garlic. Rub the mixture all over the fish heads. Season with salt and pepper.

Place the fish heads on a rimmed baking sheet. Try to keep the fish heads standing upright rather than lying on their sides. Roast for 10 minutes. (If you cannot get the heads to remain upright and they are lying on their sides, flip them after 5 minutes.)

Meanwhile, whisk together the soy sauce, honey, vinegar, orange juice, and sriracha in a small bowl to make the glaze.

Remove the pan from the oven and turn the oven temperature down to 350° F. Brush the glaze liberally over both heads and return them to the oven. Roast until cooked through, about an additional 10 minutes.

Serve the heads on a large platter.

How to Clean a Whole Fish

If you haven't ever cleaned a whole fish, don't fret. By following a few easy steps, and with some practice, you can easily add this to your fish cooking arsenal. Always try to eat or freeze fish within a day or two of bringing it home.

What You Need

When you bring home a whole fish, you'll need a few tools to make the job a little easier: a sturdy pair of kitchen shears, a small sharp knife, and a regular table knife—the kind you have in your silverware drawer.

Step One. If you are cooking the fish whole, trim the fins so they do not burn while cooking. Use the scissors to trim them down—don't completely remove them. The dorsal fin can be sharp and spikey, so be careful when cutting it. Some fish also have a sharp spike next to the anal fin; trim that as well.

Step Two. Remove all the scales: Using the table knife, start at the tail end and rub aggressively toward the head to remove the scales. Spend a few extra minutes making sure you get them all. Trouble spots are the underside of the fish, along the dorsal fin, and near the collar. Remember, be thorough: One scale is too many.

Step Three. If the guts are still in the fish, remove them after you've scaled the fish. Use your sharp knife and insert it into the anal end of the fish. Carefully break through the skin, then slide the knife toward the head. Cut straight between the pectoral fins until you reach the gills. Use your hands to pull out the guts, but be careful; try not to break or cut through anything. (Leaving the stomach intact makes it a cleaner job.) You can use your scissors to help cut away pieces that are still inside after the bulk of the guts have been removed.

Step Four. Rinse the fish under cold water to remove loose scales and clean the body cavity. If cooking right away, pat dry with paper towels. If storing in your refrigerator, wrap the whole fish in plastic so the skin does not dry out.

Grilled Fish Tails with Salsa Verde

I love cooking fish tails. I use tails from larger fish, ranging from about 10 to 15 pounds. Make sure the tails are scaled, and trim the ends of the tail fins with scissors. I usually cut the tail off just below the anal fin, slicing right through the spine. Of course, you can ask your fishmonger to do this for you. Fish tails are meant to be shared and make a great interactive communal meal when accompanied by a few sides, like Grilled Corn Salad (page 211) and Lentil and Rice Pilaf (page 220). To eat these, use a fork and knife to pull the meat from the bones, and don't be afraid to use your hands to get the last delicious bits.

Heat a grill to high heat.

In a small bowl, stir together the canola oil, garlic, shallot, and rosemary. Rub the mixture all over the outside of the fish tails. Just before cooking, season the tails with salt and pepper.

Place the tails on the hot grill. After 2 minutes, give the tails a quarter turn, then wait 2 more minutes; flip the tails over. Repeat the quarter turn method until the flesh is opaque. The process should take 8 to 10 minutes total. Remove the tails from the grill and squeeze the lemon wedges over them before serving. Serve with salsa verde on the side.

(If you don't have a grill, you can roast the tails in a 400° F oven for 15 to 20 minutes; turn the tails over once about halfway through.)

Salsa Verde

Place all ingredients except for the salt and pepper in the bowl of a food processor fitted with the metal blade and puree until smooth; season with salt and pepper to taste.

SERVES 2 TO 4

¼ cup canola oil

1 tablespoon minced garlic

1 tablespoon minced shallot

1 teaspoon minced rosemary leaves

2 trimmed and scaled fish tails from 10- to 15-pound fish

Kosher salt and freshly ground black pepper

4 lemon wedges

¾ cup Salsa Verde (below)

FOR THE SALSA VERDE

MAKES ABOUT ¾ CUP

2 cups flat-leaf parsley leaves

½ cup extra-virgin olive oil

1 clove garlic

1 teaspoon finely grated lemon zest

2 tablespoons freshly squeezed lemon juice

2 teaspoons capers, rinsed and drained

2 teaspoons Dijon mustard

½ anchovy filet, drained, rinsed, and cut into 2 pieces

¼ teaspoon red pepper flakes

Kosher salt and freshly ground black pepper

Fried Whole Black Bass with Bok Choy and Mushrooms

SERVES 2 AS AN ENTRÉE

4 heads baby bok choy

4 ounces shiitake mushrooms

¼ cup canola oil, plus more for frying

1 teaspoon chopped garlic

1 teaspoon grated ginger

2 cups Mushroom Stock (page 231)

2 whole black sea bass, about 1¼ pounds each, cleaned (for instructions, see page 151)

2 cups rice flour

Kosher salt and freshly ground black pepper

Finely grated zest and juice of 1 lime

1 tablespoon chopped cilantro

½ cup Togarashi Aïoli (page 225)

Black sea bass are wild East Coast fish that thrive up and down the coastline. They have become a recreational fish as well as a popular commercial species. You can usually find those that weigh around 1 to 2 pounds at the fish market, but there are also larger ones weighing as much as 5 pounds. For this recipe, I like using a countertop fryer that's big enough to hold at least 1 whole small fish. You can also roast the fish in the oven or grill them whole. The fish tastes great any way you prepare it, but the presentation of a whole fried fish is a showstopper.

Remove the root ends of the bok choy heads to separate the leaves. Cut off the leafy greens and set aside. Slice the thicker stem ends of the bok choy into thin strips.

Remove the stems from the shiitake mushrooms and slice the caps into thin strips.

In a large sauté pan, heat the ¼ cup canola oil over medium heat. Sauté the shiitake slices until they begin to crisp. Add the bok choy stem slices and sauté with the mushrooms until they begin to color lightly. Drain off any excess oil and stir in the bok choy greens, along with the garlic and ginger. Add the stock and simmer for 1 to 2 minutes. Remove the pan from the heat and set aside.

Line a large plate with paper towels. Fill a countertop fryer with oil and heat to 350° F. Score each fish on one side by making four deep vertical cuts along the length of the fish. Place the rice flour in a large shallow bowl. Roll the fish in rice flour to coat on all sides and shake off any excess. Carefully lower one fish into the oil—try to place it in a swimming position so that it curls a bit and cooks evenly. Fry the fish until fully cooked, about

12 minutes. To check whether the fish is fully cooked, pull back a piece of skin on the scored side and look at the flesh. Once the fish is fully cooked, remove it to the prepared plate and season generously with salt and pepper. Repeat with the second fish.

To serve, place the bok choy mixture over medium heat and add the lime juice. Once warmed through, spoon the mixture into a large shallow serving dish. Place the fish on top and garnish with the cilantro and lime zest. Serve the aïoli on the side for dipping.

Whole Grilled Bronzini with Roasted Cauliflower and Carrots

SERVES 4 AS AN ENTRÉE

2 cups cauliflower florets

4 tablespoons (½ stick) unsalted butter, melted

Kosher salt and freshly ground black pepper

4 medium carrots

¼ cup extra-virgin olive oil

1 lemon

4 whole bronzini, about 1 pound each, scaled and gutted

2 garlic cloves, thinly sliced

1 shallot, sliced

4 sprigs rosemary

3 tablespoons canola oil

1 cup arugula leaves

The fish commonly known as bronzini are usually farm-raised. Though in the past they were grown mainly in Europe, lately, we've been coming across this variety domestically as well, and what we're finding is consistently good. Bronzini are white fish that have a mild, slightly sweet flavor. One is usually the perfect size for a single person to eat whole. Make sure to request your bronzini scaled, with guts removed and fins trimmed. Always pat the fish dry with a paper towel before getting ready to cook. A clean and hot grill will help prevent fish from sticking. On the grill, use two large metal spatulas, which will make it easier to move the fish around the grates.

Preheat the oven to 375° F.

On a rimmed baking sheet, toss the cauliflower with the melted butter. Season with salt and pepper. Roast in the oven until the cauliflower is tender and begins to brown, 10 to 15 minutes. Remove and set aside to cool. Leave the oven on.

Meanwhile, peel the carrots and cut into 4- to 5-inch lengths. Cut the thick end of the carrot into 4 long pieces and the thinner end in half. On another rimmed baking sheet, toss the carrots with 2 tablespoons of the olive oil. Season with salt and pepper and roast in the oven until tender but not mushy, about 11 minutes. Set the carrots aside to cool. Reserve any olive oil that remains on the baking sheet and combine it with the remaining 2 tablespoons olive oil. Leave the oven on.

Cut the lemon in half lengthwise. Slice one half into 4 half circles. Cut the other half into wedges. Pat the bronzini dry, then stuff the belly of each fish with a lemon half circle, about one quarter each of the garlic and shallots, and 1 rosemary sprig.

Brush both sides of the fish with the canola oil and season with salt and pepper.

Heat a grill to high heat.

Thoroughly clean your grill grates. Carefully place the bronzini on the hot grill and cook for 3 minutes. Use two spatulas to carefully spin each fish a quarter turn. Repeat 2 more times on that side, then flip the fish and repeat the entire process on the other side. Cook for about 3 minutes after each spin. If your grill is really hot, you may have to move the bronzini more frequently. Remove them from the grill once they are cooked through.

To serve, place the cauliflower and the carrots back in the oven for about 5 minutes to warm them up, then arrange the vegetables on four plates. Place a fish next to each portion of vegetables. Garnish with the arugula, then drizzle the remaining olive oil and juice from the lemon wedges over the fish.

MONOMOY SPORTFISHING

Finding a Balance
with Wild and Farmed Fish

Sustainability in seafood can be a deeply complicated topic. It's really hard to make a completely sustainable choice when buying seafood, because there is so much that goes into it. I try not to make choices based on what is being called "the most sustainable" or what is on some list that attempts to tell me what to buy or where to purchase it. Instead, I try to make responsible choices based on the information I have.

Fishing for a living is one of the hardest jobs you can take on. The same goes for raising shellfish or fin fish on a farm. Every year, it seems that fishermen come under more and more pressure, what

with catch limits, regulations, and area closures. It's hard to get all of the groups that have a stake in the process to agree on anything, especially since there are so many things to measure: stock assessment, environmental impact, type of fishing equipment used, bycatch, and more. On top of that, fishermen are on the frontlines of feeling the impact of climate change and are constantly adjusting to the changes they're seeing directly on the water each day.

While many dwell on the negatives surrounding the seafood industry, I'd rather celebrate its successes. Fishermen, as I've come to understand,

have no desire to catch all the fish in the ocean. In fact, most fishermen are stewards of the sea—they hope that there will be fish for generations to come. And while they continue to work hard to make their living on the water, the industry also continues to evolve, and seacoast communities are learning to thrive by harvesting the water in different ways.

Fish farming has gotten a bad reputation for good reason. We hear about overcrowded ocean pens; negative impact on local species; pollution; antibiotic use; and farmed fish escaping into wild ecosystems. All of that understandably gives us pause when choosing farmed fish. But to be clear, many of these issues are just as prevalent in land-based agriculture. Words like "free range," "grass fed," "hormone free," and "organic" might make us feel better about what we are buying, but they don't always paint the most accurate picture. The same goes for seafood. Two of the most consumed seafood species in

America are shrimp and salmon—and most of what we see of those two species are imported and farmed. As consumers, we need to educate ourselves and make the choices that feel best for us.

One of the first things to understand is that the fisheries off the coasts of the United States are the most well-managed in the world. That means that when a piece of seafood is labeled as being from the United States, you can rest assured that it was caught within stock limits and from a reliable source.

Meanwhile, farmed seafood is not always bad. In fact, sometimes it's better than wild. When done right, fish farming puts less pressure on the oceans to supply wild seafood. And it's going to be essential as we try to feed our expanding population. Globally, aquaculture is a 200-billion-dollar industry that will only continue to grow in the foreseeable future.

Today, there's been great progress in farmed seafood systems. All aquaculture programs have pros and cons, but it's an industry that's constantly progressing. Now, we're seeing closed systems, open ocean pens, submergible pens, and many more options. Shellfish farming is undergoing innovation every day at the ground level and has a positive impact on our oceans.

Knowing what I know now, I tend to think of fish farms like vegetable farms; there are small farms that responsibly grow seafood, and there are large farms that are trying to squeeze as much money out of the product as possible. Just understand that some have better practices than others and the ways they choose to raise their products ends up impacting the quality. The best thing you can do is learn more about these systems and decide which ones make the most sense for you.

I was fortunate to learn about aquaculture by working with the University of New Hampshire. The university was growing steelhead trout, mussels, and kelp in an integrated multi-trophic aquaculture (IMTA) system, which is essentially a system in which multiple organisms are grown together. The program uses an open ocean pen anchored off the New Hampshire coast.

Inside the university's IMTA, you'll find steelhead growing in the interior of the pens while mussels and kelp grow vertically around the exterior. There are many reasons for growing all three together. The fish create nitrogen by producing waste, but the mussels and kelp help filter nitrogen out of the water. The mussels also remove sea lice (an issue for fish in warmer months) from the water surrounding the pen. The fish (all females that come from a nearby hatchery) convert their feed into protein rather quickly; plus they're marketable, versatile, and tasty. The system provides not only diverse crops, but also a well-balanced, mutually beneficial ecosystem that has little to no impact on the environment.

Once I got to know this method for growing steelhead trout, I realized it fit into my sensibility—it was a method of fish farming that I could really get behind. It seemed like a logical approach to balancing some of the issues that come with fish farming, especially since the University of New Hampshire had the added goal of inviting local fishermen to participate in the farming process; something like this set up as a co-op might be a way to continue to help seacoast communities. For now, whether it becomes a long-term money maker or a scalable system remains to be seen, but the program and others like it are definitely making progress.

Since then, I've tried to learn more about different fish farming methods. I occasionally buy fish from a recirculating aquaculture system (RAS), and while the flavor might not be as bright as that of wild fish, the process continues to get better. There are now open ocean pens and different closed systems that are gaining momentum. How the world perceives these methods remains to be seen—by supporting domestic aquaculture and trying new fish, you're continuing to help the industry improve. Don't let "farmed" on a seafood label stop you from buying fish.

Striking a balance between buying farmed and wild seafood is an important part of the success of both industries. Supporting small, local fisheries is always my first choice but not always the most practical when shopping or writing menus. By maintaining that balance, I feel good about my choices, and about what will ultimately land on the plate.

CHAPTER FIVE

Composed Dishes

Summer Tomatoes with Burrata and Grilled Bread

SERVES 4 AS AN APPETIZER

6 slices sourdough bread

¼ cup extra-virgin olive oil

4 medium beefsteak tomatoes, washed and cored

One 4-ounce ball burrata

1 cup medley tomatoes

1 tablespoon balsamic vinegar

Kosher salt and freshly ground black pepper

12 small basil leaves

It's hard to find anything better than a summertime, sun-ripened tomato. There are so many varieties these days, and I like them all, but my favorite is a regular old red beefsteak tomato with a little salt and olive oil sprinkled over the top. The beauty of good tomatoes is that they need very little help to taste good. Medley tomatoes are grape and cherry tomatoes in a mix of colors, often heirloom varieties. Slice them at the last minute so they stay juicy. Burrata and grilled bread are the perfect partners to summer tomatoes—just be sure to use really good-quality olive oil and vinegar. And, if you don't have a grill, feel free to toast the bread in the oven instead.

Heat a grill to medium-high heat.

Brush the bread slices on one side with 2 tablespoons of the olive oil and place them on the grill, oiled sides down. Cook until they get a light, evenly colored char, moving them frequently. Cut the grilled bread in half and set aside.

Slice the beefsteak tomatoes into ¼-inch slices and arrange them on a large plate, overlapping slightly. Place the burrata in the center of the tomatoes. Halve the small tomatoes and scatter them around the plate. Drizzle the vinegar and remaining 2 tablespoons olive oil over all the tomatoes and season generously with salt and pepper. Garnish with the basil leaves and serve with the grilled bread.

Smoked Haddock Hash with Bacon, Poached Egg, and Hollandaise

I love when rustic ingredients come together in a dish. You can replace hollandaise with Salsa Verde (page 153) or Basil Pesto (page 223), or use smoked trout instead of haddock.

Place potato cubes in a medium saucepan and cover with cold, salted water. Bring to a simmer and cook until tender. Drain the potatoes and spread out on a baking sheet or tray to cool.

Line a plate with paper towels. In a large sauté pan, heat 1 tablespoon of the canola oil over medium-high heat and add the diced bacon. Cook until the bacon is crisp, then transfer to the prepared plate.

Add the remaining 2 tablespoons canola oil to the pan. Place over medium heat and add the red onion, red pepper, and celery; sauté until they begin to color lightly. Remove the pan from the heat and season with salt and pepper. Stir in the crisp bacon.

In another large sauté pan, melt the butter over medium-high heat until it begins to brown slightly. Add the potatoes and paprika and cook until the potatoes are hot and lightly browned. Pour off any excess butter. Add the potatoes to the vegetable and bacon mixture.

In a medium saucepan, bring 2 cups of water and the distilled vinegar to a simmer; the liquid should not be boiling. Crack each egg into a small bowl, then gently slip them into the water and poach them for 4 minutes.

While the eggs are poaching, place the vegetable and potato mixture back over medium heat to warm it through. Use your hands to flake the smoked fish into pieces. Add the fish to the pan along with the scallions, gently folding everything together. Season the mixture with salt and pepper. To serve, divide the mixture between two bowls and place a poached egg on top of each portion. Add a spoonful of hollandaise over each egg and serve hot.

SERVES 2 FOR BREAKFAST OR BRUNCH

1 cup cubed (unpeeled) red potato

Kosher salt

3 tablespoons canola oil

½ cup diced slab bacon

¼ cup diced red onion

¼ cup diced red bell pepper

¼ cup thinly sliced celery

Freshly ground black pepper

3 tablespoons unsalted butter

¼ teaspoon paprika

1 tablespoon distilled white vinegar

2 large eggs

12 ounces Smoked Haddock (page 68)

2 scallions, thinly sliced

¼ cup Hollandaise Sauce (page 46)

Bay Scallops with Roasted Sweet Potato and Brown Butter

SERVES 4 AS AN APPETIZER

1 sweet potato

¼ cup kosher salt plus more to taste

¼ cup canola oil

1 teaspoon chopped garlic

1 tablespoon chopped shallot

¼ cup dry white wine

1 cup heavy cream

¼ cup Vegetable Stock (page 230)

Freshly ground black pepper

1 pound bay scallops

2 tablespoons unsalted butter, softened

¼ teaspoon finely grated lemon zest

¼ teaspoon freshly squeezed lemon juice

1 tablespoon chopped flat-leaf parsley leaves

Bay scallops differ from sea scallops in size and also the location where they are harvested: smaller bay scallops are harvested near the shore in a bay, while sea scallops are harvested further out in the sea and are much larger. I love both, but here in New England one of the many joys of autumn is getting locally caught wild bay scallops. They are harvested for only a few weeks off of Cape Cod, Nantucket, and Martha's Vineyard. It's a romantic scene as a fisherman heads out in waders to a small bay along the coast and rakes scallops, then carefully places them in a basket. The reality? It's freaking cold and a lot of work. Bay scallops are worth the price, and they're easily one of the best-tasting products harvested from any ocean.

Preheat the oven to 350° F.

With the tip of a paring knife or a fork, pierce the sweet potato skin all over. Pile the ¼ cup of salt on a baking sheet and place the potato on top. Bake in the oven until completely cooked through, about 50 minutes.

While the potato is baking, heat 2 tablespoons of the canola oil in a medium skillet over medium heat. Add the garlic and the shallot and sauté until they begin to color lightly. Add the white wine and reduce until almost gone. Add the cream and reduce by half. Remove from the heat and keep the cream in the skillet.

When the potato is fully cooked, remove it from the oven and cut it in half. Scoop out the flesh and place it in the skillet with the reduced cream. Add the stock and season with salt and pepper. Return the skillet to the heat and bring the cream–sweet potato mixture to a gentle simmer, stirring frequently. Remove from the heat and spoon the mixture into a blender or the bowl of a food processor fitted with the metal blade and puree until smooth.

Pat the scallops dry with a paper towel and season with salt and pepper. Heat the remaining 2 tablespoons canola oil in a medium skillet. Once the oil is hot, add the scallops, making sure not to overcrowd the pan. (You may need to do this in batches.) Sear the scallops for 30 seconds. Holding the scallops in place with a spoon or spatula, pour off any excess oil that remains in the pan. Add the butter to the pan and cook until the butter and scallops brown; be sure to shake the pan frequently. Just before serving, add the lemon zest, juice, and parsley to the scallops.

To serve, spread the warm puree on a serving dish and use the back of a spoon to create a well for the scallops. Spoon the scallops and butter sauce onto the puree and serve warm.

Brown Rice Crab Bowls with Snap Peas and Fried Eggs

At Row 34, this dish is hugely popular, especially at lunch. Loaded with vegetables and a little bit of heat, it's a great way to show off good quality crabmeat. At home, it's easy to work into your lunchtime routine, too, especially if you do all the prep work and chopping ahead of time. I always recommend splurging on good crabmeat; fresh is always best, though there are good pasteurized options out there, too. If you can't find crab, shrimp or lobster will also shine in this dish.

In a medium saucepan, combine the rice and 1 cup water. Season with salt. Bring to a simmer, lower the heat, and cover. Simmer until the rice is tender, about 20 minutes. If needed, drain the rice, then spread it out on a plate or baking sheet to cool.

In a medium bowl, combine the lime juice, vinegar, sriracha, sesame oil, and sesame seeds. Whisk to combine and set aside.

Remove the ends from the sugar snap peas and pull the string that runs along the edge of each shell. Slice the peas into ¼-inch-thick pieces on a 45-degree angle. Chop off the root end of the bok choy to separate the leaves. Leave the leafy parts of the leaves whole and thinly slice the thicker stalks.

In a large nonstick skillet, heat 2 tablespoons of the canola oil over medium-high heat. Add the ginger, garlic, and scallion whites and sauté until they just start to color. Add the sliced bok choy stalks, onion, carrot, and red pepper, and cook for 2 minutes, stirring frequently. Add the cut snap peas and the whole bok choy leaves; sauté for 1 additional minute.

Stir in the cooled rice and the stock. Cook until the mixture is hot throughout and the liquid is mostly absorbed.

SERVES 2 AS AN ENTRÉE

½ cup uncooked short- or medium-grain brown rice

Kosher salt

1 tablespoon freshly squeezed lime juice

2 teaspoons rice wine vinegar

2 teaspoons sriracha hot sauce

2 teaspoons sesame oil

1 teaspoon black sesame seeds

18 sugar snap peas

1 head baby bok choy

3 tablespoons canola oil

1 teaspoon grated fresh ginger

1 teaspoon minced garlic

2 scallions, thinly sliced, white and green parts separated

¼ cup diced onion

¼ cup diced carrot

¼ cup diced red bell pepper

¼ cup Vegetable Stock (page 230)

6 ounces crabmeat, preferably fresh, picked through for shells

Freshly ground black pepper

2 large eggs

Gently fold in the crabmeat and season with salt and pepper. Divide between two serving bowls.

Wipe out the skillet with a paper towel. Place the remaining 1 tablespoon canola oil in the skillet over medium heat. Crack the eggs into the pan and cook until the whites are firm but the yolks are still runny.

Top each serving with a fried egg. Whisk the lime-sesame sauce briefly to combine, then drizzle over both bowls. Garnish with the sliced scallion greens.

Baked Bluefish with Fennel and Spring Garlic

I love changing people's mind about bluefish. Most people are put off by bluefish because they regard it as having a strong "fishy" flavor, but when handled correctly, bluefish is delicious. It's truly one of my favorites. This is a "gateway" bluefish recipe that uses the whole filets. Ask your fishmonger to leave the skin on as it makes the fish easier to handle but trim out all the bones. And, if you're a griller, you can also cook these filets in their foil pouch on a charcoal grill with a few wood chips thrown onto the fire.

Preheat the oven to 350° F.

Line a baking sheet that's big enough to fit the filets with two layers of aluminum foil, letting it hang over the edges by several inches. Using two separate pieces of foil is fine. Brush a little olive oil on the foil. Using a paper towel, pat the bluefish filets dry. Cut each filet into 2 pieces, then arrange the pieces flat, skin-side down, on the foil. Season with salt and pepper.

In a medium bowl, stir together the fennel, red onion, spring garlic, tarragon, sherry vinegar, and the remaining olive oil. Season with salt and pepper, then spoon the mixture evenly over the bluefish filets.

Fold up the foil around the filets and crimp the edges to seal so that the fish will steam inside the foil packet. Place the baking sheet in the oven and bake for 15 minutes. Remove and carefully open the foil; the steam will escape, so use caution. Using the bottom piece of foil, or a fish spatula, carefully slide the filets and vegetables onto a serving platter. Squeeze the lemon wedges over the fish. (When eating the fish, remove it from the skin in pieces, leaving the skin behind.)

SERVES 4 AS AN ENTRÉE

¼ cup extra-virgin olive oil

2 bluefish filets with skin, about 2¼ pounds

Kosher salt and freshly ground black pepper

1 cup shaved fennel

½ cup shaved red onion

¼ cup thinly sliced spring garlic (see Chef's note below)

1 teaspoon chopped fresh tarragon

3 tablespoons sherry vinegar

4 lemon wedges (see page 43)

Chef's note: Spring garlic—known as green garlic in some places—has a robust flavor. Clean it as you would a leek or scallion and use both the white and green parts. If you can't find spring garlic, use a little chopped regular garlic instead.

Grilled Salmon with Creamy Dill Cucumbers

SERVES 4 AS AN ENTRÉE

3 cups peeled, seeded, and sliced
   English cucumbers

1 tablespoon chopped dill

1 teaspoon cider vinegar

¼ cup crème fraîche

¼ cup very thinly sliced red onion

Kosher salt and freshly ground
   black pepper

4 skinned salmon filets, about
   6 ounces each

2 teaspoons canola oil

4 lemon wedges

This combination of rich salmon with cool, crisp cukes is sure to become a summertime staple. Dill cucumbers are delicious and easy to make—eat them with the salmon or on their own. I prefer crème fraîche in them, but you can use sour cream instead. Whether you grill the salmon over wood or charcoal—my preference—or on a gas grill, don't over-heat it: you want the grill hot enough to give the fish some color but not so hot that it chars the flesh. I tend to move the fish around the grill to find the sweet spot. Personally, I like to cook salmon so that it's warmed all the way through but not well done.

In a large bowl, stir together the cucumbers, dill, vinegar, crème fraîche, and red onion. Season with salt and pepper and refrigerate until ready to serve.

Preheat a grill to medium heat.

Using a paper towel, pat the salmon filets dry. Brush each filet with ½ teaspoon canola oil and season with salt and pepper. Place the filets on the grill, on what would have been skin-side down, and cook for 2 minutes. Using a spatula, give the fish a quarter turn and cook 2 minutes more. Repeat two more times for a total of 8 minutes. The goal is to evenly cook and color each piece of fish. Flip the fish over and cook for another 2 to 3 minutes. Remove from the grill and squeeze a lemon wedge over each salmon filet.

Serve the cucumbers on the side.

Pan-Roasted Fluke with Lentil and Rice Pilaf

SERVES 4 AS AN ENTRÉE

SERVES 4 AS AN ENTRÉE

4 skinned fluke filets, about 6 ounces each

Kosher salt and freshly ground black pepper

3 tablespoons canola oil

3 tablespoons unsalted butter, softened

2 tablespoons minced shallot

¼ cup dry white wine

1 tablespoon freshly squeezed lemon juice

1 tablespoon chopped chives

1 tablespoon chopped flat-leaf parsley leaves

1 batch Lentil and Rice Pilaf (page 220)

Fluke is also called summer flounder, and it's pretty common along the East Coast. It's a flat, lean white fish that is firm when cooked. The filets are perfectly sized for pan roasting. Try to cut your portions from the thickest parts of the filet. (And be sure to save the ends, which make excellent ceviche or crudo; see Fluke Crudo with Lemon Oil, Charred Scallions, and Pistachio on page 90.) Be sure to use a pan that will fit all of the fluke, or cook this in two batches and wait to make the pan sauce after the second batch. I like to serve this with Garlicky Green Beans (page 209).

Using a paper towel, pat the fluke filets dry, then season with salt and pepper. In a sauté pan that's large enough to hold all of the filets (or cook in two batches), heat the canola oil over medium heat. Carefully arrange the fluke filets in the pan with what would have been the skin-side up.

Sauté the fish until it begins to color lightly around the edges, about 3 minutes. Using a fish spatula, carefully flip the fish. Add 2 tablespoons of the butter to the pan; once the butter has melted, tilt the pan toward you and use a spoon to baste the fish until it cooks through. The total cooking time will be about 5 minutes.

Remove the fish from the pan and set aside. Pour out about half of the fat from the pan, then add the shallot and return to medium heat. Sauté until the shallot just begins to color. Add the white wine and increase the heat to bring to a boil; lower the heat and simmer until the liquid is almost gone. Stir in the lemon juice and remaining 1 tablespoon butter. Keep stirring until the butter melts, then add the chives and parsley.

Arrange the fluke on a serving platter along with the pilaf. Pour the sauce over the fish and rice.

Grilled Swordfish with Horseradish Butter and White Beans

Swordfish is built for grilling. Be sure to find pieces that are thick—if they're too thin, they overcook easily. Make the beans in advance—it will be easier to assemble the dish as you start grilling. If you don't have cannellini beans, you can use chickpeas here instead.

About 1 hour before you plan to cook the swordfish, in a small bowl stir together 3 tablespoons olive oil with the garlic, paprika, and lemon zest. Place the fish on a baking sheet or tray and rub the mixture on all sides of the swordfish. Refrigerate until ready to grill.

Heat the grill to medium-high heat.

Remove the swordfish from baking sheet, letting the excess marinade drain off the fish. Season each piece with salt and pepper. Place the swordfish on the grill and cook for 2 minutes before giving the pieces a quarter turn. If the flames flare up, move the fish to a different spot. Repeat the quarter turns until the swordfish has cooked for 6 minutes on one side. Flip the fish and cook for an additional 4 minutes on the other side. The fish should be warm all the way through. Just before removing the fish from the grill, top each piece of fish with a slice of the horse-radish butter and let it melt for a few seconds before removing the fish from the grill.

In a large sauté pan, heat the remaining 2 tablespoons olive oil. Add the leek and shallot and sauté until they just start to soften. Add the cooked beans and diced tomato. Bring the mixture to a simmer, then add the parsley and season with salt and pepper. To serve, spoon the bean mixture into four shallow serving bowls and place a piece of swordfish on top of each portion.

SERVES 4 AS AN ENTRÉE

¼ cup plus 1 tablespoon extra-virgin olive oil

1 teaspoon minced garlic

¼ teaspoon paprika

½ teaspoon finely grated lemon zest

4 swordfish steaks, about 7 ounces each

Kosher salt and freshly ground black pepper

4 thin rounds Horseradish Butter (page 226), at room temperature

1 small leek, split, rinsed, and white parts thinly sliced

1 tablespoon minced shallot

2 cups White Beans (page 179), drained

1 beefsteak tomato, core removed and diced

2 tablespoons chopped flat-leaf parsley leaves

White Beans

Rinse the beans under cold water, then place in a large bowl and add cold water to cover by a few inches. Refrigerate overnight.

Drain and rinse the beans, then place them in a medium stockpot. Add cold salted water to cover and bring to a boil. Meanwhile, gather the rosemary, thyme, garlic clove, peppercorns, and bay leaf in a coffee filter; use twine to tie the filter's top closed, making a bundle.

Once the beans have come to a boil, remove the pot from the heat, drain the beans in a colander, then return the beans to the pot. Add the stock and the herb bundle to the stockpot. Bring everything back to a boil, then turn down to a simmer. Let the beans simmer until they are tender but not mushy, about 1 hour. Remove the stockpot from the heat and let the beans cool in the liquid. Remove and discard the herb bundle.

FOR THE WHITE BEANS

MAKES ABOUT 2 CUPS

1 cup dried cannellini beans

Kosher salt

1 sprig rosemary

1 sprig thyme

1 clove garlic

4 whole black peppercorns

1 bay leaf

4 cups Vegetable Stock (page 230)

Monkfish Cutlets and Spaetzle with Swiss Chard

SERVES 2 AS AN ENTRÉE

½ cup canola oil

2 monkfish filets, about 5 ounces each, well-trimmed

½ cup unbleached all-purpose flour

1 large egg

1 cup panko breadcrumbs, ground fine in a food processor

1 teaspoon mustard powder

½ teaspoon paprika

¼ teaspoon ground turmeric

Kosher salt and freshly ground black pepper

1 batch Spaetzle with Swiss Chard (opposite)

1 cup Beurre Blanc (page 225)

Monkfish are as ugly as they get—but the filets have beautiful, firm white flesh. Monkfish has become more commonly available, and for good reason: it's versatile and tasty. It's usually caught year-round, but I tend to look for it in the wintertime when other species aren't as readily available. When you pound the monkfish filets, try not to make them too thin, otherwise it's easy to overcook them. Make the Spaetzle with Swiss Chard before you do anything else. Cooking the fish should be the last thing you do before assembling the plates.

Cut two pieces of plastic wrap, each about 10 by 10 inches. Spread one on a hard surface and very gently brush the plastic with a little of the canola oil. Place one of the monkfish filets in the center and place the other piece of plastic on top. With a meat mallet or rubber mallet, gently pound the monkfish until it is an even ½ inch thick. Set that filet aside and repeat with the other filet.

Place the flour in a shallow bowl. In another shallow bowl, beat the egg. In a third shallow bowl, mix together the breadcrumbs, mustard powder, paprika, and turmeric. Season each monkfish filet with salt and pepper, then dredge each piece of filet in the flour, shaking off any excess.

Transfer the filets to the bowl with the egg and coat well, letting any excess drip off. Lastly, place the filets into the breadcrumbs. Gently press the filets against the breadcrumbs so that all sides are well-coated.

In a large sauté pan, heat the remaining canola oil over medium-high heat. Once the oil is hot, place the monkfish filets in the pan. Cook until they start to turn golden brown on the bottom.

Lower the heat, then carefully flip the filets and continue cooking on the other side until golden brown. Remove the pan from the heat and remove the monkfish to a paper towel–lined plate to drain.

Divide the spaetzle between two plates. Place a monkfish filet on top of each portion. Spoon the beurre blanc around the plates.

Spaetzle with Swiss Chard

In a medium bowl, stir together the flour, salt, and pepper. In another bowl, whisk together the milk, eggs, and mustard. Add the wet ingredients to the dry ingredients and stir until smooth.

Fill a large stockpot about ¾ of the way full with water. Bring to a boil. Set a colander over the pot. Slowly pour the batter into the colander and use a rubber spatula to press the batter through the colander holes into the water. The batter will break into droplets that will float. Simmer for 3 minutes. Using a slotted spoon, scoop out the spaetzle and spread on a baking sheet or tray to cool.

In a large sauté pan, heat the canola oil over medium heat. Add the onion and cook until it starts to soften. Add the Swiss chard leaves and cook until the leaves wilt. Once wilted, pour the contents of the pan into a medium bowl and return the pan to the heat. Add the butter to the pan. Once the butter has melted and is starting to bubble, add the cooked spaetzle; fry the spaetzle in the butter until they just begin to color lightly.

Drain off any excess butter from the pan and add the Swiss chard back to the pan with the spaetzle. Cook until the mixture is heated through and well combined. Taste and season with salt, black pepper, and the lemon juice.

FOR THE SPAETZLE WITH SWISS CHARD

MAKES ABOUT 2 CUPS

1 cup unbleached all-purpose flour

1 teaspoon kosher salt

¼ teaspoon ground white pepper

¼ cup whole milk

2 large eggs

1 tablespoon grain mustard

2 tablespoons canola oil

½ cup sliced yellow onion

2 cups torn red Swiss chard leaves, thick ribs removed

2 tablespoons unsalted butter

Freshly ground black pepper

2 teaspoons freshly squeezed lemon juice

Roasted Pollock with Braised Tomatoes and Pearl Pasta

SERVES 4 AS AN ENTRÉE

2 tablespoons kosher salt, plus more for seasoning

2 teaspoons ground turmeric

1½ cups pearl pasta

¼ cup extra-virgin olive oil

1 tablespoon chopped garlic

2 tablespoons minced shallot

3 cups medley tomatoes, halved

Freshly ground black pepper

10 basil leaves

2 or 4 skinned pollock filets, 2 pounds total

2 tablespoons canola oil

1 teaspoon finely grated lemon zest

½ teaspoon curry powder

¼ cup minced red onion

Pollock from the West Coast is the most harvested wild fish on the planet. If you've ever had fish sticks or a fast food fish sandwich, you've eaten West Coast pollock. It's also an East Coast species that is a member of the cod family. When we went fishing as kids, we would bring a few home to my grandmother, who would cook them as a special treat for the cats. Thankfully, we soon figured out that pollock is delicious for humans, too. Whether you're getting East or West Coast pollock, this recipe is a good way to show off the fish's texture and flavor. Pearl pasta is also called Israeli couscous; adding a little bit of turmeric amps up the flavor and makes a visually beautiful dish.

Preheat the oven to 400° F.

In a medium saucepan, combine 3 cups water, the 2 tablespoons salt, and the turmeric and bring to a rolling boil. Add the pearl pasta, stir, and reduce the heat to low. Simmer until tender, 10 to 12 minutes. Once the pasta is cooked, drain and set aside to cool.

Place a large sauté pan over medium heat. Add the olive oil and the garlic; when the garlic just begins to color, add the shallot and tomatoes. Cook the mixture gently over low heat until the tomatoes soften and their juice starts mixing with the olive oil, about 15 minutes. Season with salt and pepper. Add the pearl pasta to the sauté pan, increase the heat to medium, and stir to combine. Tear the basil leaves and fold into the mixture. Remove from the heat and set aside until ready to serve.

Using a paper towel, pat the pollock filets dry. Season them with salt and pepper. Brush a baking sheet with a little of the canola oil and arrange the pollock filets on the sheet, folding the

tail-end of each piece under the filet so that it doesn't burn. In a
small bowl, stir together the remaining canola oil with the lemon
zest, curry powder, and red onion; spoon this mixture over the
pollock filets. Place the baking sheet in the oven and roast for
8 minutes.

To serve, spoon the pearl pasta onto a serving dish. Place the
roasted pollock on top of the pearl pasta and spoon any juices
remaining on the sheet pan over the fish. Serve hot.

Bucatini with Littlenecks

Clams and pasta are about as classic a pairing as you can get. Plump and briny littlenecks are one of my favorite shellfish, but it's easy to overcook them, and in this dish there's little for them to hide behind. While you're cooking the clams, be sure to remove them from the pan as soon as they open. Make sure your clams are washed really well before starting out. If you'd like, add a basket of grilled bread to the table for soaking up the delicious juices. I prefer freshly made pasta with this dish. If you have a local pasta shop that makes fresh bucatini, source it from them. Most any dry pasta works well though, but just be sure to adjust your cooking time as needed.

In a large stockpot, bring 1 gallon (16 cups) of water and the 2 tablespoons salt to a boil. This salty water will be used to cook the pasta and should be ready to go before you start cooking the clams, especially if you are using fresh pasta, which takes only a few minutes to cook.

Place the clams, wine, bay leaves, and thyme in a medium saucepan or Dutch oven that has a tight-fitting lid. Bring to a boil and then reduce to a simmer. Cover and simmer until all the clams open. Discard any closed clam shells.

Use a slotted spoon to remove each clam from the pan as it opens, transferring them to a large bowl. After removing all the clams, remove the pan from the heat and let the liquid cool a little. Carefully pour the liquid slowly into another bowl or container, letting any sand that may have come out of the clams while cooking stay in the bottom of the pan. Discard the thyme and bay leaves.

2 tablespoons kosher salt, plus more to taste

24 littleneck clams, cleaned (see page 41)

1 cup dry white wine

2 bay leaves

2 sprigs thyme

1 pound bucatini or other long pasta

3 tablespoons extra-virgin olive oil

1 shallot, minced

3 garlic cloves, minced

3 tablespoons unsalted butter

Freshly ground black pepper

1 tablespoon freshly squeezed lemon juice

¼ cup roughly chopped flat-leaf parsley leaves

1 teaspoon red pepper flakes

Cook the pasta in the boiling water until al dente, then drain in a colander.

In a large sauté pan, heat the olive oil over medium heat and add the shallot and garlic. Sauté until they just begin to color; add the reserved clam cooking liquid and bring to a boil. Stir in the butter until it melts and quickly add the pasta and clams, tossing gently to combine. Season with salt and pepper and stir in the lemon juice.

Place the pasta and clams in a large serving bowl, pulling a few clams out to arrange on top. Garnish with parsley and red pepper flakes.

Baked Steelhead Trout with Grain and Apple Salad

A steelhead trout starts its life in freshwater as a rainbow trout; if it migrates to saltwater, it then becomes a steelhead trout. Most of the steelhead available these days is farm raised in a way that makes it a smart choice for the dinner table. The texture is similar to that of Arctic char or salmon, but it has its own unique flavor. Cook the barley and the lentils in advance; if you're unsure how to cook lentils, follow the instructions in the pilaf recipe on page 220.

In a medium saucepan, combine the stock with the barley and season with salt. Simmer over medium-high heat until the barley is tender, about 15 minutes. Drain off any excess stock and spread the barley on a baking sheet to cool.

Cut the apple into 4 pieces, core it, then thinly slice each quarter. Place the apple slices in a large salad bowl, along with the watercress. Dress the greens and apple with 2 tablespoons of the vinaigrette and toss.

Once the barley is cool, add it to the salad bowl, along with the cooked lentils. Gently toss the barley salad together and season with salt and pepper.

Preheat the oven to 325° F.

Prepare a baking sheet by brushing the oil on the surface. Using paper towels, pat the steelhead filets dry and arrange the pieces on the oiled baking sheet. Season each piece with salt and pepper. In a small bowl, stir together the shallot, olive oil, and lemon zest; spoon over the filets. Bake in the preheated oven for 14 to 16 minutes depending on the thickness of the filet.

To serve, pile the salad onto a serving dish. Place the filets on top of the salad and serve the remaining vinaigrette on the side.

SERVES 4 AS AN ENTRÉE

2 cups Vegetable Stock (page 230)

½ cup pearl barley

Kosher salt

1 small apple, preferably Fuji

1 cup baby watercress

6 tablespoons Harissa Vinaigrette (page 228)

¾ cup cooked lentils

Freshly ground black pepper

2 teaspoons canola oil

4 skinned steelhead trout filets, about 6 ounces each

1 tablespoon minced shallot

2 tablespoons extra-virgin olive oil

2 teaspoons finely grated lemon zest

Flounder with Anchovy Butter

SERVES 4 AS AN ENTRÉE

8 skinned flounder filets, about 3 ounces each

1 tablespoon canola oil

¼ cup Vegetable Stock (page 230)

Kosher salt and freshly ground black pepper

8 thin rounds Anchovy Butter (page 227)

2 tablespoons chopped chives

4 lemon wedges (see page 43)

Don't overlook, or undervalue, a good piece of flounder. This fish is usually inexpensive and always easy to cook—plus, it's delicious. There are many varieties of flounder and all will work well with this recipe. The anchovy butter really brings this together. I like to make a meal out of this by serving it with Lentil and Rice Pilaf (page 220) and Grilled Corn Salad (page 211).

Preheat the oven to 350° F.

Loosely fold the head and tail ends of each flounder filet underneath the fish so that they meet in the middle. Brush a baking dish with the canola oil. Place the flounder filets in the dish, keeping the ends folded; there should be a little space between each filet. Pour the stock around the filets; it should just cover the bottom of the baking dish. Season the filets with salt and pepper.

Place one round of butter on top of each filet (see page 162). Bake in the preheated oven for 12 to 16 minutes depending on the thickness of the filet.

Remove the baking dish from the oven and spoon the melted butter back over the filets. Garnish the filets with the chopped chives and serve the lemon wedges on the side.

Seared Halibut with Tomatoes, Olives, and Capers

You can find halibut on both coasts: On the West Coast, it's referred to as Alaskan halibut; on the East Coast, it's just halibut. Both work for this recipe. Halibut is a lean fish and can easily be overcooked—your cooking time will vary depending on the thickness of the fish. I like it warmed all the way through to the center. This is a dish made for summer, because it depends on sun-ripened, just-picked tomatoes. I like using the mixed small tomatoes sold as medley tomatoes, so that there are several different colors and varieties on the plate.

Preheat the oven to 350° F.

Using a paper towel, pat each halibut filet dry and season with salt and pepper. In a large, ovenproof sauté pan, heat the canola oil over medium-high heat. Add the halibut to the pan. Sear on one side until it just begins to color, 2 to 3 minutes. Carefully turn the fish over and transfer the pan to the oven. Roast for 7 minutes.

Meanwhile, in a medium sauté pan, warm the olive oil over medium heat, then stir in the garlic. Once the garlic begins to sizzle, add the tomatoes. Heat the tomatoes until they just begin to release their juices. Remove the pan from the heat and stir in the olives and capers.

Just before serving, tear the basil leaves and stir them into the tomatoes and season with salt and pepper. Place the halibut filets on a platter and evenly spoon the tomatoes over the top.

SERVES 4 AS AN ENTRÉE

4 skinned halibut filets, 6 ounces each

Kosher salt and freshly ground black pepper

3 tablespoons canola oil

½ cup extra-virgin olive oil

1 teaspoon chopped garlic

2½ cups medley tomatoes, halved

2 tablespoons sliced Kalamata olives

1 teaspoon capers, rinsed, drained, and coarsely chopped

12 basil leaves

Dijon and Parsley–Crusted Cod with Turmeric Rice

SERVES 4 AS AN ENTRÉE

½ cup panko breadcrumbs

1 cup flat-leaf parsley leaves

Kosher salt and freshly ground black pepper

2 teaspoons canola oil

4 skinned cod filets, 7 ounces each

1 tablespoon Dijon mustard

½ cup Beurre Blanc (page 225)

Asparagus from page 208, omit the onion and feta

2 cups Turmeric Rice (page 220)

I highly recommend the book *Cod: A Biography of the Fish That Changed the World* by Mark Kurlansky. Every time I prepare cod, I can't help thinking of his book and cod's influence on the world. While Kurlansky can explain the fish better than I can, I would argue that I'm probably better at cooking it. This preparation can also be done with haddock, hake, or even salmon—but try it at least once with cod and consider the rich history behind it. As much as you may love mustard, don't be tempted to double up on the Dijon as it can quickly overpower the fish. To round out the meal, serve this with asparagus (see instructions on page 208) and Turmeric Rice (page 220).

Preheat the oven to 350° F.

Place the breadcrumbs and parsley in a food processor and pulse; the crumbs will take on a greenish color. Season with salt and pepper.

Prepare a baking sheet by brushing it with the oil. Place the cod on the oiled sheet and pat each portion dry with a paper towel. Season with salt and pepper. Lightly brush the mustard on top of each piece and then sprinkle the breadcrumbs on top of the mustard. Bake for 15 minutes. Carefully transfer the fish to a serving dish and serve the beurre blanc, asparagus, and rice on the side.

Seared Scallops with Mushrooms and English Peas

Morel mushrooms are one of the true gems of spring. Their arrival means that the season is changing and that we can start cooking in new ways. They are easily my favorite mushrooms, but if you can't find morels, almost any other mushroom will be great in this dish. I like to get a good sear on my mushrooms and then finish them with a little butter. I've made many variations of this dish over the years and it continues to be one of my favorites.

Remove the stems from the mushrooms and cut each one in half from the tip toward the stem end. Plunge the mushrooms into a bowl of water and stir them around to remove any dirt or sand. Do not let them sit in the water; quickly move them around and then remove from the water. Repeat this step three times, using fresh water each time; let the mushrooms dry on paper towels.

In a medium sauté pan, heat 2 tablespoons of the canola oil over medium-high heat. Add the mushrooms and cook until the moisture has cooked out of them and they begin to get a good sear. Drain any excess oil from the pan and return the pan to the heat. Add half of the butter and the sliced garlic to the pan. Sauté until the garlic wilts and the mushrooms get a little more color from the butter. Remove from the heat and set aside.

Fill a medium saucepan with cold, salted water and bring to a boil. Quickly blanch the peas in the water for a few minutes, then drain well. Add the peas to the pan with the mushrooms, along with the thyme leaves and lemon zest, and fold everything together.

In another sauté pan, heat the remaining 2 tablespoons canola oil over medium-high heat. Pat the scallops dry with a paper towel and season lightly with salt and pepper. Once the oil is hot, add them to the pan. Sauté the scallops until they have good

SERVES 2 AS AN ENTRÉE

1 cup morel mushrooms

¼ cup canola oil

1 tablespoon unsalted butter

1 tablespoon sliced spring garlic (see Chef's note, page 173)

Kosher salt

½ cup shelled English peas

¼ teaspoon thyme leaves

1 teaspoon finely grated lemon zest

14 ounces (about 8) sea scallops

Freshly ground black pepper

2 teaspoons freshly squeezed lemon juice

1 cup Beurre Blanc (page 225)

brown color on the bottom. Carefully turn the scallops over. Add the remaining butter to the pan and use a spoon to baste the scallops with the hot oil and butter. Remove the pan from the heat and drizzle the lemon juice over the scallops. Place the pan with the mushrooms over medium heat and reheat until just warmed through. To serve, divide the mushroom mixture between two plates. Place the scallops on top and drizzle the beurre blanc around each plate.

Rosemary Roasted Chicken with Mashed Potatoes and Garlicky Green Beans

Like most people, I love a good roasted chicken. There is something particularly satisfying and nurturing about it. It's a simple dish, yet when done right it can be a very memorable meal. At Row 34, we think it's important to have a few delicious "from the land" dishes on the menu, sprinkled among all of the seafood—I want to make sure that everyone who comes through our doors can find something good to eat.

Preheat the oven to 500° F.

With a sharp, stout knife, butterfly the chicken by removing its backbone. Place the bird on a cutting board, then split the breastbone so that the bird lies flat. Carefully remove the breastbone, wish bone, and rib bones from inside the chicken. The only bones remaining should be the leg, thigh, and wing bones. Make sure the skin stays intact and covers the chicken.

In a blender, puree the 2 garlic cloves with the roughly chopped shallot, canola oil, 4 tablespoons of the butter, and rosemary until smooth. Rub the mixture all over the skin of the chicken. Liberally season the bird with salt and pepper.

Set the chicken on a rimmed baking sheet, skin-side up. Place it in the oven and roast for 15 minutes. Remove the pan from the oven and lower the temperature to 325° F. Return the pan to the oven and continue to roast until the chicken is golden and the juices run clear, basting now and then with any fat or juices that accumulate on the baking sheet, about 30 to 45 additional minutes.

Meanwhile, place the remaining 3 tablespoons melted butter in a small saucepan over medium heat. Add the remaining garlic and shallots and cook until just softened but before they start

SERVES 4 AS AN ENTRÉE

1 whole chicken, 3 to 4 pounds

2 cloves garlic, plus 1 teaspoon chopped

1 shallot, roughly chopped, plus 1 tablespoon diced

¼ cup canola oil

1 stick butter, melted

2 tablespoons rosemary leaves, lightly chopped

Kosher salt and freshly ground black pepper

2 tablespoons all-purpose flour

1½ cups chicken stock

2 tablespoons flat-leaf parsley leaves, chopped

½ lemon

1 batch Mashed Potatoes (following page)

1 batch Garlicky Green Beans (page 209)

2 large russet potatoes, peeled
and cut into 2-inch pieces

Kosher salt

¾ cup heavy cream

3 tablespoons unsalted butter,
softened

2 tablespoons sour cream

1 tablespoon chopped chives,
optional

Freshly ground black pepper

to color. Add the flour and stir constantly until the flour smooths out. Whisk in the chicken stock and continue whisking while bringing the sauce to a simmer. Once the sauce is smooth, lower the temperature to very low heat and continue cooking for 10 more minutes. Strain the sauce through a fine-mesh strainer and season with salt and pepper; keep warm. Add the parsley right before serving.

Increase the oven temperature back to 500°F and roast the chicken for 5 minutes more to crisp up the skin. Watch carefully so that it doesn't burn. Once crisped, remove the chicken from the oven and let it rest for 10 minutes. Squeeze the lemon half over the entire chicken before serving.

To serve, use a sharp knife to slice the chicken breast away from the bone, then separate the wings, legs, and thighs. Serve with the sauce, potatoes, and green beans on the side.

Mashed Potatoes

Preheat the oven to 300°F.

Place the potatoes in a large saucepan and add cold salted water to a cover. Bring to a simmer over medium-high heat and cook until potatoes are tender but not mushy. Drain well, then spread the potatoes on a baking sheet. Place in the oven to dry, about 5 minutes. Run the potatoes through a ricer or food mill into a large bowl.

Place the cream and butter in a small saucepan and heat over medium heat until simmering. Fold the hot cream mixture into the potatoes. Finish by stirring in the sour cream and chives, if using. Season with salt and pepper. Keep warm until ready to serve.

Marinated Skirt Steak with Tomatoes and Blue Cheese

This combination of steak and tomatoes makes for a casual summer meal. Skirt steaks are sometimes cut thin; if so, adjust the cooking time so you don't overcook the meat.

In a blender, puree ¼ cup of the oil, orange zest and juice, shallot, garlic, red pepper flakes, and cumin until smooth.

Using paper towels, pat the steaks dry. Place the steaks in a casserole dish and pour the marinade over the top, turning and flipping the meat so that all sides are coated. Cover and refrigerate for 1 hour.

Meanwhile, preheat the oven to 350° F.

On a baking sheet, toss the red onion with 1 tablespoon of the olive oil and bake for 10 minutes. Remove and let cool.

Core the Early Girl and yellow tomatoes, then cut them into wedges and cut the wedges in half. Place in a large bowl with the roasted onions, arugula, medley tomatoes, sherry vinegar, and remaining 3 tablespoons olive oil. Toss gently and season with salt and pepper. Set aside until ready to serve.

Heat a grill to high heat.

Remove the skirt steaks from the marinade and place on the grill. Cook the steaks, moving them occasionally, for about 4 minutes. Flip the meat and continue to cook for another 2 minutes. Remove from the grill, season with salt and pepper, and let the steaks rest for 5 minutes. Toast the sourdough slices on the grill. Cut each slice in half.

To serve, spread the tomato mixture on a platter. Thinly slice the steaks at an angle against the grain and place the pieces over the tomatoes. Sprinkle the crumbled blue cheese on top and serve the grilled sourdough bread on the side.

SERVES 4 AS AN ENTRÉE

½ cup extra-virgin olive oil

1 teaspoon finely grated orange zest

2 tablespoons freshly squeezed orange juice

1 shallot, chopped

2 cloves garlic

½ teaspoon red pepper flakes

¼ teaspoon ground cumin

4 skirt steaks, 7 ounces each

1 red onion, cut into ½-inch slices

2 Early Girl tomatoes

2 yellow tomatoes

2 cups arugula leaves

1 cup medley tomatoes, halved

3 tablespoons sherry vinegar

Kosher salt and freshly ground black pepper

4 slices sourdough bread

½ cup crumbled blue cheese

Butterscotch Pudding with Whipped Cream and Candied Pecans

MAKES SIX 8-OUNCE SERVINGS

2 sheets gelatin

8 ounces butterscotch chips

6 egg yolks

2 tablespoons scotch

¼ cup light brown sugar

3½ cups heavy cream

2 teaspoons vanilla extract

½ teaspoon sea salt

2 cups Whipped Cream (opposite)

½ cup Candied Pecans (opposite)

FOR THE WHIPPED CREAM

MAKES ABOUT 2 CUPS

1 cup heavy cream

1 teaspoon pure vanilla extract

1 tablespoon confectioners' sugar

FOR THECANDIED PECANS

MAKES ABOUT ½ CUP

½ cup sugar

¼ cup shelled pecans

A great dessert is often one that has a powerful nostalgia factor that brings you to another time and place in life. For me, butterscotch does that—it's a flavor from my childhood that is simple yet satisfying at the same time. I've been making this dessert for years. I brought it to Boston from the restaurant I worked at in California, and it's been popular at every restaurant that's served it. The recipe has changed a bit over the years, but I've always used real scotch. Now, it's a tried-and-true staple at Row 34—and hopefully will be in your home, too.

In a large bowl, submerge the gelatin in cold water until it blooms, 5 to 10 minutes. Drain the liquid, wringing any additional liquid from the sheets, and return the gelatin to the empty bowl. Place the butterscotch chips in the bowl.

Place the egg yolks in a medium bowl. In a medium saucepan, combine the scotch and the brown sugar and bring to a boil while stirring constantly. Add the cream, vanilla, and salt and return to a boil. Temper the eggs by adding a little of the hot cream mixture to the egg yolks and whisking vigorously. Pour the tempered eggs into the saucepan with the cream mixture and cook over medium heat, whisking constantly, until the mixture thickens enough to coat the back of a spoon.

Pour the hot cream mixture over the butterscotch chips and gelatin; whisk until all of the chips are melted and the mixture is smooth. (A handheld immersion blender will help if you have one.)

Strain the pudding through a fine-mesh strainer and divide among six individual 8-ounce serving jars. Refrigerate for at least 6 hours. To serve place a dollop of whipped cream on top of each jar and then garnish with the pecans.

Whipped Cream

In a chilled bowl with chilled beaters or whisk, beat all ingredients together until soft peaks form. Refrigerate until ready to serve.

Candied Pecans

Place the sugar in a medium sauté pan and heat over medium heat until melted. Use a metal spoon to stir as it melts so that the sugar colors evenly. Add the pecans and stir until they are well coated. Let cool in the pan; transfer pecans to a cutting board. Use a knife or the back of a pan to chop or smash the pecans into bite-sized pieces.

Do You Know Where Your Fish Comes From?

A Conversation with Jared Auerbach of Red's Best

Jared Auerbach wants you to be optimistic about where your seafood comes from. The founder of Red's Best, a wholesale seafood distributor located on the historic 1914-built Boston Fish Pier, is well aware of the constant warnings about fish stock declines, plastics in our ocean, catch limits and regulations, and what the Monterey Bay Aquarium's Seafood Watch list has to say.

But, as he can see from his company's perch on the pier, which overlooks all of Boston Harbor, the ocean is too vast, too deep, and too unknowable for most humans to understand. "Our brains can't completely fathom all of its resources," he says, a little in awe of what the ocean holds.

What he does understand, and has built his business upon, is that the men and women who fish from it every day have a clearer vision than most of the endless cycle of the ocean's bounties. And that knowledge is incredibly valuable.

Red's Best is essentially a network of fishermen. The company finds innovative ways to match the supply of fish coming off of thousands of small-catch boats with the demands of the marketplace. After Jared founded the business in 2008, he immediately set out to create proprietary data-gathering technology that could collect small data points, like the location where a single striped bass was caught by one particular boat off the coast of Cape Cod. The technology also tracks the equipment used, the fisherman's story, and the size of the boat.

While the technology itself is exciting, the ability to track fish is now widespread. What Red's brings to the table is the ability to aggregate that information. One fisherman might catch one fish, but by aggregating the information from hundreds of small boats catching the same type of fish in one day, Red's is able to offer a large market presence. Once the fish are unloaded at the dock, Red's takes control, managing the fish from dock to market. At the processing facility on the Boston Fish Pier, an army of fish cutters and packers manage the fish, labeling every piece with a QR code for the buyer. This way, the fishermen can keep fishing (instead of worrying about where to sell their fish); their catch and stories are collected; and Red's does the work of selling as much of the fishermen's catch as possible.

Along the way, Jared is able to connect consumers to their fishermen. "We all want to be connected to a real community, to the stories," he says.

What's more, Red's is now partnered with universities and other large institutions, like Harvard, to provide large-scale fish CSAs. Like a farmer's CSA on steroids, Red's delivers thousands of pounds of fish to a school or institution each week, depending on what's coming off the dock. So, students might be eating sea bass one week and hake the next—and all of it serves the fishermen making the catch.

Jared is proud of Red's niche in the industry. "We're able to harvest this wild, mysterious, unknown natural resource in a sustainable way and feed a lot of people with it. And it's mostly from small mom-and-pop businesses," he says. "What we're doing is making sure real money is going to a family in our community. And that is nourishing even more of our community."

When I first opened my restaurants, I made the decision to write the menus each day—after opening I realized that was maybe my best or worst decision. But it enables me to look at what's coming off the boats, rather than, say, make up a menu based on my whims and not mother nature's. Not every species of fish will be available every day. Instead of committing to a certain type of fish on my menu, I am supporting local fishermen and what they are catching. Being flexible is important when cooking in a restaurant or at home.

I couldn't have done this without Red's Best. With their technology, I can see exactly what's available off the water that day—and it almost always opens up possibilities in terms of what to prepare. It might be monkfish and redfish one day, and salmon the next. Whatever it is, I've trained everyone in the kitchen to be flexible, to utilize the entire fish, and to think in terms of what we can do with what's available, rather than demanding something that's not.

Jared and I probably have different definitions of what sustainability means when it comes to seafood. But I know that both of us are committed to the sustainability of the industry. We're devoted to our local fishing communities and committed to putting fishermen first.

Sides, Sauces, and Staples

Asparagus with Roasted Onions

SERVES 4 AS A SIDE DISH

1 large red onion, sliced

¼ cup extra-virgin olive oil

Kosher salt and freshly ground
    black pepper

2 teaspoons freshly squeezed
    lemon juice

1 teaspoon Dijon mustard

2 bunches asparagus

½ cup crumbled feta cheese
    (optional)

This dish is good at room temperature or warm. Look for larger asparagus spears, and peel the stem about halfway up the stalks. Larger asparagus will take a little longer to cook but the size makes for a great presentation. To prep this in advance, cook and shock the asparagus ahead of time.

Preheat the oven to 400° F.

On a baking sheet, toss the sliced red onion with 2 tablespoons of the olive oil and season with salt and pepper. Roast in the oven for 5 minutes. Set aside to cool.

In a small bowl, whisk together the lemon juice and Dijon mustard. Add the remaining 2 tablespoons olive oil in a thin stream, whisking constantly, and continue whisking until combined.

Trim the bottom third off of each asparagus spear. Use a peeler to peel the tough outer layer from the bottom half of each stalk. Bring a large saucepan of salted water to a boil. Add the asparagus and blanch in the boiling water for 4 minutes. Drain and place the asparagus on a serving platter. Season with a little salt, then drizzle the Dijon dressing over the asparagus. Top with the roasted onions and the feta, if using.

Roasted Potatoes

SERVES 4 AS A SIDE DISH

½ cup extra-virgin olive oil

2 tablespoons rosemary leaves

6 large fresh sage leaves

2 large cloves garlic

2 pounds fingerling potatoes

Kosher salt and freshly ground
    black pepper

2 tablespoons chopped flat-leaf
    parsley leaves

I love roasted potatoes. Fingerlings work well here, but feel free to use your favorite small potato; just be sure to wash them well and leave the skin on.

Preheat the oven to 375° F.

Place the olive oil, rosemary, sage, and garlic in a blender and puree until smooth.

Cut the potatoes in half lengthwise. In a large bowl, toss the potatoes with the oil mixture. Season with salt and pepper and spread on a baking sheet in an even layer. Bake the potatoes in the preheated oven until tender, about 35 to 40 minutes, shaking the pan occasionally and adding more oil as desired. Transfer to a serving dish and garnish with chopped parsley.

Garlicky Green Beans

A little bit of finely grated garlic, butter, and lemon juice turn these basic beans into a bright, savory side dish.

Set up a bowl of ice water. In a large stockpot, bring 1 gallon (16 cups) of salted water to a boil. Add the beans and simmer until tender but not too soft (they should still have a little snap), about 6 minutes. With a slotted spoon or skimmer, transfer the green beans to the ice water bath to stop the cooking process. Drain the green beans once they're cool.

Place the butter in a large sauté pan. Use a microplane to grate the garlic over the butter, then place the pan over low heat. When the butter has melted and the garlic starts to sizzle, add the olive oil to the pan. Raise the heat to medium-low. Add the beans to the pan and increase the heat to medium. Toss the beans with the garlic mixture to coat well; cook until the green beans are heated through. Off the heat, add the lemon juice and season with salt and pepper. Serve hot.

SERVES 4 AS A SIDE DISH

Kosher salt

1 pound green beans, trimmed

2 tablespoons unsalted butter

2 large cloves garlic

2 tablespoons extra-virgin olive oil

2 teaspoons freshly squeezed lemon juice

Freshly ground black pepper

Avocado and Sesame Salad

Ripe avocados are the key to this recipe. If they start to break down a little and look creamy while mixing, that's ok. If you make this ahead, place the salad in an airtight container, press a piece of plastic wrap against the surface, cover with the lid, and refrigerate to keep the avocados from turning brown.

Slice the avocados in half lengthwise and remove the pits. Carefully scoop the flesh from the skin using a spoon, then cut into about 1-inch dice. Place in a medium bowl and sprinkle with the lime juice. Peel the cucumber, cut in half lengthwise, and remove the seeds. Slice the cucumber thinly, then add it to the avocado. Fold in the red onion, rice wine vinegar, and sesame oil and season with salt and pepper. Toss a few times to combine. Place in a serving bowl and garnish with the sesame seeds, radish slices, and parsley.

SERVES 4 AS A SIDE DISH

3 ripe avocados

1 tablespoon freshly squeezed lime juice

1 English cucumber

½ small red onion, halved or quartered and thinly sliced

2 tablespoons rice wine vinegar

1 tablespoon toasted sesame oil

Kosher salt and freshly ground black pepper

½ teaspoon black sesame seeds, toasted

½ teaspoon white sesame seeds, toasted

1 red radish, sliced into thin rounds

1 tablespoon roughly chopped flat-leaf parsley leaves

Coleslaw

MAKES ABOUT 4 CUPS

1 cup distilled white vinegar

1 cup sugar

½ teaspoon cayenne pepper

1 tablespoon mustard seeds

1 tablespoon celery seeds

1 tablespoon whole black
    peppercorns

6 cups shredded green cabbage

1 cup shredded carrot

1 cup mayonnaise, plus more as
    needed

1 cup sour cream, plus more as
    needed

Kosher salt and freshly ground
    black pepper

This coleslaw is a classic companion to any type of fried fish and will be a great addition to your next summer cookout. I like it on top of a fish or chicken sandwich as much as I like it alone.

In a medium saucepan, combine the vinegar, sugar, cayenne, mustard seeds, celery seeds, and black peppercorns. Bring to a boil, then remove from the heat and let sit for 1 hour. Strain and discard the solids and let the liquid cool completely. Refrigerate until ready to use.

Place the cabbage and carrot in a large mixing bowl and pour the cooled vinegar mixture over the top; toss well to combine. Stir in the mayonnaise and sour cream; season with salt and pepper. Let sit for about 10 minutes; the cabbage will begin to wilt. Mix again and adjust the seasoning and the amount of mayonnaise and sour cream, if necessary: the coleslaw should be very well coated in the dressing but not swimming in it. Refrigerate until ready to serve. Just before serving toss again to coat evenly with the dressing.

Brown Butter Cauliflower

SERVES 4 AS A SIDE DISH

1 small head cauliflower

1½ sticks (12 tablespoons)
    unsalted butter

1 teaspoon thyme leaves

1 tablespoon freshly squeezed
    lemon juice

Kosher salt and freshly ground
    black pepper

Cauliflower and brown butter are made for each other. The butter will brown with the cauliflower as it cooks in the oven; carefully baste the cauliflower by spooning the butter from the baking sheet back over the top.

Adjust an oven rack to the middle position and preheat the oven to 500° F.

Remove the core from the head of the cauliflower and cut the head into florets. The florets should be no more than 2 inches wide or long. Place the florets in a large bowl. Melt the butter in a saucepan and cook until foaming subsides. Pour the melted butter over the florets and toss until well-coated. Spread the cauliflower on a large rimmed baking sheet. Place the sheet in the center of the oven and roast for 6 minutes. Stir the florets and baste them with the butter, then lower the heat to 375° F and cook for 8 minutes more.

Remove the pan and toss the cauliflower with thyme leaves and lemon juice. Season with salt and pepper. Serve immediately.

Grilled Corn Salad

This dish should be on the table as often as possible during the summer. As with all recipes, using fresh ingredients is the key here—and good summer corn is hard to beat. If you don't want to grill the corn, you can shave it off the cob and then sauté it with the rest of the vegetables. You could also switch out tarragon for basil or oregano, depending on what's fresh.

Heat a grill to medium-high heat.

Brush the corn with the canola oil and season with salt and pepper. Place the cobs on the hot grill, rotating frequently to get an even color all around. You want a little char on the corn, but be careful not to let it burn. Remove the corn and set aside until cool enough to handle. Once cool, shave the kernels off of the cob.

In a sauté pan, heat the olive oil over medium heat, then add the garlic. Once the garlic just starts to brown, add the bell pepper, red onion, and white parts of the scallion. Sauté for 1 minute, stirring frequently. Add the corn kernels and cook until everything is warmed through, about 3 minutes. Remove from the heat and stir in the tarragon and lemon juice. Season with salt and pepper. Garnish with the green slices of scallion.

SERVES 4 TO 6 AS A SIDE DISH

- 6 ears corn, husked and silks removed
- 2 tablespoons canola oil
- Kosher salt and freshly ground black pepper
- 3 tablespoons extra-virgin olive oil
- 2 cloves garlic, chopped
- 1 red bell pepper, cut into small dice
- 1 small red onion, cut into small dice
- 4 scallions, thinly sliced, white and green parts separated
- 1 tablespoon chopped tarragon leaves
- 1 tablespoon freshly squeezed lemon juice

Spicy Cucumbers

This side dish is easy to make, and it tastes great on its own or as a part of a meal. The peanuts are optional—they add crunch, but the dish works just as well without them. If you want to omit the spice, you can make this without the jalapeño and/or the red pepper flakes.

Use a peeler to peel off 4 to 5 strips of the cucumber skin down the length of each cucumber, leaving a few strips of the peel intact. Cut the cucumber in half lengthwise and use a spoon to gently scrape out the seeds. Cut each piece in half lengthwise again, and then into 1-inch pieces.

In a mixing bowl, toss the cucumbers with the jalapeño, pickled onions, lime juice, and olive oil, and season with salt and pepper. Place the cucumbers in a serving dish and top with the red pepper flakes, mint, and peanuts before serving.

SERVES 4 AS A SIDE DISH

- 2 English cucumbers
- 1 small jalapeño, seeded and minced
- ¼ cup Pickled Red Onions (page 215), drained
- 2 tablespoons freshly squeezed lime juice
- 3 tablespoons extra-virgin olive oil
- Kosher salt and freshly ground black pepper
- 1 teaspoon red pepper flakes
- 6 small mint leaves, sliced
- 3 tablespoons toasted peanuts, crushed

Roasted Brussels Sprouts with Bacon and Parmesan

1½ pounds (about 6 cups) Brussels sprouts, trimmed and halved

3 tablespoons canola oil

Kosher salt and freshly ground black pepper

6 slices bacon, cut into ½-inch pieces

2 cloves garlic, chopped

1½ tablespoons sherry vinegar

Finely grated zest of 1 lemon

¼ cup finely grated Parmesan cheese (grated on a microplane)

I don't know when Brussels sprouts started to take over as everyone's favorite vegetable, but I have always loved them. Really large Brussels sprouts might need to cook a little longer. Save the large outer leaves that fall off when you're trimming the sprouts—you can fry them up and use them as a tasty bonus garnish.

Preheat the oven to 450° F.

On a baking sheet, toss the Brussels sprouts with the canola oil and season with salt and pepper. Spread evenly, then bake for 15 minutes. The sprouts should be tender but not mushy.

Meanwhile, in a skillet large enough to fit the Brussels sprouts, sauté the bacon over medium-high heat until crisp. Drain off all but 2 tablespoons of the bacon fat, leaving the bacon in the pan. When the sprouts are out of the oven, add the garlic to the pan with the bacon, then add the Brussels sprouts. Sauté everything together until the sprouts are coated with bacon and garlic. Remove from the heat, then toss with the sherry vinegar, lemon zest, and more salt and pepper to taste. Transfer to a serving dish and sprinkle the Parmesan on top.

Creamy Mushrooms

Different mushrooms cook at different speeds, so I chose cremini mushrooms for this dish because they cook consistently, they're almost always available, and they're tasty. If you don't have sherry vinegar, you can use a little drop of lemon juice for the acid, which helps smooth out the richness of this dish.

Trim the ends of the mushroom stems but leave the stems attached. Rinse the mushrooms under cool water to remove any dirt. Let dry on a paper towel. Cut the mushrooms into quarters.

In a large sauté pan, heat the butter over medium heat. Add the garlic and shallots and cook until they just begin to color lightly. Add the mushrooms and stir to coat with the butter mixture. Sauté until the moisture from the mushrooms cooks off, 8 to 10 minutes. Add the wine and bring to a simmer. Add the cream and thyme leaves. Let the mixture simmer until the sauce has reduced enough so that it coats the back of a spoon; it should not be too thick. Stir in the sherry vinegar, then season with salt and pepper. Transfer to a serving bowl and garnish with chives.

SERVES 4 AS A SIDE

1 pound cremini mushrooms

3 tablespoons unsalted butter

2 cloves garlic, minced

2 large shallots, minced

½ cup dry white wine

1½ cups heavy cream

1 teaspoon fresh thyme leaves

2 tablespoons sherry vinegar

Kosher salt and freshly ground
    black pepper

1 tablespoon chopped chives

Crispy Shallots

This is an easy recipe, and these go great with raw fish. Use a mandoline to slice the shallots very thin and evenly, and pay attention at the end of the cooking process, as the shallots go from crisp to burnt very quickly. The leftover oil is great for vinaigrettes and marinades.

Set a colander or large strainer over a large heatproof bowl. Line a plate with paper towels. Use your hands to gently separate the shallots into rings. Place the shallots in a large saucepan and cover them with the oil. Place the pan over medium heat and heat until little bubbles start to form and boil around the shallots. Lower the heat and gently stir every few minutes. The shallots will start to color; keep stirring frequently. Once they are an even brown color, quickly remove the pan from the heat and strain the shallots in the prepared colander or strainer, reserving the oil for another use.

Spread the shallots on the prepared plate and season with salt. They will last for a few days stored in an airtight container at room temperature.

MAKES ABOUT 1 CUP

2 large shallots, thinly sliced

4 cups canola oil

Kosher salt

Pickled Vegetables

MAKES ABOUT 3 CUPS

1 to 2 large carrots

1 fennel bulb, fronds and core removed

1 red onion

¼ cup (¼-inch-strips) red bell pepper

2 radishes, thinly sliced

1 clove garlic

1½ cups cider vinegar

¾ cup sugar

1 teaspoon mustard seeds

1 teaspoon whole black peppercorns

1 teaspoon fennel seeds

1 tablespoon kosher salt

This recipe makes a great basic hot pickle and it works with all kinds of vegetables. Experiment with whatever is in season or in your refrigerator. I like putting these out with just about any smoked fish dish or serving them with grilled bread as an easy rustic appetizer.

Using a mandoline or vegetable slicer, shave the carrot, fennel, and onion into thin slices. You should have about 1 cup carrot, ½ cup fennel, and ½ cup red onion. Place the carrot, fennel, red onion, bell pepper, radishes, and garlic in a 16-ounce glass jar or one that is large enough to hold them all. They can be packed in the jar, but there should be enough room to add the pickling liquid.

In a small saucepan, combine the vinegar, sugar, mustard seeds, black peppercorns, fennel seeds, and salt and bring to a rolling boil. Remove from the heat and stir until the sugar is fully dissolved. Strain the liquid and pour it over the vegetables in the jar. Let the liquid cool to room temperature, then seal the jar with the lid and refrigerate. These will keep in the refrigerator for up to 6 days.

Bread and Butter Pickles

MAKES ABOUT 4 CUPS

3 pounds pickling cucumbers, sliced ¼-inch thick

¼ cup kosher salt

3 cups ice

1 yellow onion, peeled and thinly sliced

2 cups distilled white vinegar

1½ cups sugar

1 tablespoon ground turmeric

1 teaspoon celery seed

½ teaspoon ground white pepper

1 tablespoon yellow mustard seeds

1 teaspoon red pepper flakes

Pickles are easy to make and they're a great thing to have in the refrigerator. If you like sweet over spicy, omit the red pepper flakes. I like these on almost any sandwich.

Place the sliced cucumbers and the salt in a colander set in a large bowl. Top the cucumbers with the ice and let drain in the refrigerator for 1 to 3 hours. Once drained, remove any excess ice and divide the cucumber slices and onion slices between two tall 1-quart glass jars.

Combine the remaining ingredients in a medium saucepan and bring to a boil. Pour the boiling liquid over the cucumbers and onions, filling both jars. Let the liquid cool to room temperature, then seal the jars and refrigerate. Let sit for at least 8 hours before serving. These will keep in the refrigerator for up to 2 weeks.

Pickled Red Onions

This super simple recipe can be pretty versatile—put these zingy onions on a sandwich or toss them into salads. They'll keep in an airtight container in the refrigerator for up to two weeks.

Cut the onions in half and remove the root ends. Thinly slice the onions into half-moons and place in a large mixing bowl. Stir in the sugar, vinegar, and salt. Let sit at room temperature for about 30 minutes, stirring every few minutes. Eventually the onions will begin to wilt and the liquid will cover the onions.

Cover and refrigerate until ready to use. Drain the pickled onions briefly before using.

MAKES ABOUT 2 CUPS

2 medium red onions

½ cup sugar

½ cup champagne vinegar

1 teaspoon kosher salt

Curried Chickpeas

This is a dish that gets better on the second day. You can substitute canned chickpeas, but the flavor is much better when all the ingredients cook together. I like to pair this with seared scallops (page 195) or grilled salmon (page 174).

In a large saucepan, heat the canola oil over medium heat. Add the onion and garlic and sauté until they begin to color. Add the curry powder and drained chickpeas and stir until combined. Add the stock and bay leaves and season with salt.

Simmer until the chickpeas are tender, about 40 minutes. Remove the saucepan from the heat and place ½ cup of the chickpeas and 1 cup of the cooking liquid in a blender. Puree until smooth and then add the puree back to the cooked chickpeas in the saucepan.

Add the carrot and celery to the saucepan, return to medium-high heat, and bring to a simmer. Simmer until the vegetables have softened slightly, then add the coconut milk and remove from the heat. Just before serving, remove and discard the bay leaves and stir in the lemon zest and juice and sriracha. Tear in the Thai basil leaves and season with salt and pepper.

MAKES ABOUT 4 CUPS

3 tablespoons canola oil

½ cup minced yellow onion

2 tablespoons minced garlic

1 tablespoon curry powder

2 cups dried chickpeas, soaked overnight, then drained

6 cups Vegetable Stock (page 230)

2 bay leaves

Kosher salt

½ cup diced carrot

½ cup diced celery

½ cup coconut milk

Finely grated zest and juice of 1 lemon

2 tablespoons sriracha hot sauce

2 tablespoons Thai basil

Freshly ground black pepper

Vegetable Chips

Homemade chips are simple. A little patience is the most important ingredient. Don't overfill your fryer and be sure to fry them long enough to become crisp. A small countertop fryer works great for many of the recipes in this book, but especially this one—follow the manufacturer's instructions if using one. These chips are great for any occasion. Be sure to salt them as soon as they come out of the oil.

4 cups canola oil

2 russet or sweet potatoes, ends trimmed and rinsed

Kosher salt

Potato or Sweet Potato Chips

Fill a large bowl with cold water. Line a large plate with paper towels. In a wide, straight-sided skillet or Dutch oven, heat the oil to 325° F. Slice the potatoes very thinly. (Use a mandoline if you have one; if not use a very sharp knife.) Place in the cold water as soon as they are sliced. When all the potatoes are sliced, drain the water and replace with fresh water. Repeat until the water is clear. Drain the potatoes well and pat them dry. Place slices in the oil one at a time until there is a layer of potatoes covering the top. (You will need to work in batches.) Stir and carefully flip potatoes so they fry on both sides. Once they are lightly browned, about 2½ minutes, remove with a skimmer and transfer to the paper towel–lined plate to drain. Immediately season with salt. Repeat until all potatoes are fried.

VARIATIONS

Taro Chips: Try to find a taro root that's about the size of a potato, as they are usually slightly larger. Peel off the dark skin and slice into thin rounds. Rinse and fry using the same method as for potatoes. Taro chips will fry in about 1½ minutes.

Lotus Chips: Use only fresh lotus root with the skin on. Peel and slice into thin rounds. Rinse and fry using the same method as for potatoes. Lotus chips will fry in about 1½ minutes.

Plantain Chips: Trim the ends and remove the skin from green plantains. Cut the plantains into 3-inch lengths and cut lengthwise into thin pieces. Do not rinse, just place the slices directly into the frying oil. Plantain chips will fry in about 2 minutes.

Grain and Arugula Salad

This dish becomes an easy, last-minute side if you cook the grains in advance—all you have to do is assemble it. Feel free to omit a grain or add your favorite to this—it's a really versatile recipe. Most grains have an earthy and sometimes rich flavor, so the arugula helps balance things out. You'll be surprised how much the orange zest adds to the dish.

Place the quinoa, barley, and brown rice in separate saucepans, and add 1 bay leaf to each. Add 1 cup stock to the quinoa and season with a pinch of salt. Bring to a boil, then quickly reduce the heat to a simmer and cover. Simmer for about 10 minutes, or until the quinoa is tender. Remove the quinoa from heat and strain off any excess liquid. Spread the quinoa on a baking sheet or tray, fluff with a fork, and let cool.

Meanwhile, add 1½ cups stock to the barley and the remaining 1 cup stock to the brown rice. Cook both until the grains are tender (times will vary) and strain off any excess liquid. Let cool to room temperature, then refrigerate until ready to assemble.

Once the grains are cool, in a large mixing bowl, combine the quinoa, barley, brown rice, and lentils. Toss in the arugula, orange zest, sherry vinegar, and olive oil and mix until the grains are well coated. Season with salt and pepper. Transfer to a serving dish and sprinkle the almonds over the top.

SERVES 4 TO 6 AS A SIDE DISH

½ cup quinoa

½ cup barley

½ cup brown rice

3 bay leaves

3½ cups Vegetable Stock (page 230)

Kosher salt

½ cup cooked red lentils (see page 220)

1 cup arugula

Finely grated zest of 1 orange

3 tablespoons sherry vinegar

¼ cup extra-virgin olive oil

Freshly ground black pepper

¼ cup almonds, toasted and chopped

242 Fries

SERVES 4 AS A SIDE DISH

6 large russet potatoes

1 cup kosher salt, plus more for seasoning

4 cups canola oil (see Frying Seafood at Home, page 15)

2 tablespoons chopped flat-leaf parsley leaves

Freshly ground black pepper

These fries became popular at my first restaurant, which was located at 242 Harvard Street, hence the name. Chef Jasper White once told me they were the best fries he had ever eaten—high praise from a New England icon. The restaurant had an amazing eleven-year run, and the fries live on. Instead of putting the potatoes in cold water and bringing them to a boil, I wait and add the potatoes once the water is boiling—this technique yields a great texture. Potatoes love salt, so don't be afraid to season these heavily.

Rinse the potatoes and cut the outside edges off on four sides so that potatoes sit flat on a cutting board. Cut each potato into 3 pieces lengthwise, and then cut each of those pieces into 3 more pieces lengthwise; you should have 9 long, thick fries from each potato. Place the potatoes in a colander and rinse them under cold water until the water runs from cloudy to clear; this will take a few minutes, so stir them up every few minutes and let the water continue to run.

Line a baking sheet with a dishtowel. In a large stockpot, combine 1 gallon of water and 1 cup salt and bring to a boil. Carefully add the potatoes to the water and boil them until they are just cooked through, about 12 minutes. Use a slotted spoon or skimmer to transfer the potatoes to the prepared baking sheet. Let the potatoes cool, and then place the whole tray in the freezer. Once frozen, the potatoes can be transferred to an airtight container and left in the freezer.

When you're ready to fry, place the oil in a large, straight-sided skillet or Dutch oven and bring to 350° F. Line a plate with paper towels. Take the fries from the freezer and, using tongs, immediately transfer them to the frying oil. Cook until the fries are golden brown and crispy, 8 to 9 minutes. Transfer the fries to the prepared plate and sprinkle with parsley. Season with salt and pepper. Serve hot.

Turmeric Rice

MAKES ABOUT 2 CUPS RICE

2 tablespoons canola oil

¼ cup minced yellow onion

2 teaspoons minced garlic

1 teaspoon ground turmeric

1 cup long-grain white rice

1½ cups Vegetable Stock
   (page 230)

1 bay leaf

Kosher salt

This is an updated version of an old-fashioned rice pilaf—I like to add garlic for flavor, as well as turmeric for vibrant color.

In a saucepan with a tight-fitting lid, heat the canola oil over medium heat. Add the onion and garlic and sauté until they just barely start to color. Stir in the turmeric and rice, add the stock, and bring to a boil. Add the bay leaf and season with salt. Turn the heat down to a gentle simmer and cover with the lid. Cook for 18 minutes, then remove from the heat and let sit, covered, for 5 minutes.

Use a fork to fluff the rice. Remove and discard the bay leaf. Either serve the rice immediately while it is still warm, or spread the rice on a baking sheet to cool; once cool, place in an airtight container and refrigerate until ready to use, then reheat before serving.

Lentil and Rice Pilaf

SERVES 4 AS A SIDE DISH

2 tablespoons canola oil

¼ cup minced yellow onion

¼ cup green lentils

¼ cup red lentils

2 cups plus 3 tablespoons
   Vegetable Stock (page 230)

2 bay leaves

Kosher salt and freshly ground
   black pepper

1 cup Turmeric Rice (see above)

1 tablespoon unsalted butter

1 teaspoon chopped dill

Red lentils cook much faster than green lentils, so keep an eye on both as they cook. If you make this in advance, you can easily pop it in a microwave to reheat it. The dill is really floral—but feel free to replace it with parsley if you feel the flavor of dill will overwhelm the other items on the menu.

Divide the canola oil into two small saucepans and place both over medium heat. Divide the onion between the two pots and sauté until it becomes translucent. Add the green lentils to one saucepan and the red lentils to the other. Add 1¼ cups of stock to the green lentils and ¾ cup of stock to the red lentils. Add 1 bay leaf to each saucepan and season with salt and pepper. Simmer the lentils until they are tender, 15 to 17 minutes for the green lentils and 5 to 6 minutes for the red lentils. Once they are tender, strain off any excess liquid and set aside until cool.

In a large bowl, combine both types of lentils with the rice. In a large sauté pan over medium heat, combine the butter with the remaining 3 tablespoons stock and cook until the butter melts. Add the lentil and rice mixture to the pan. Cook, stirring frequently. Once the mixture is hot all the way through, add the dill and season with salt and pepper.

Saltines

I love serving homemade saltines with (and crushed up in) chowder (page 110) or on the table as part of a meal. Make the dough ahead of time and break the dough up into small pieces to freeze—you can pull them out as needed. Once the sheets are baked, break them into random shapes before serving.

Preheat the oven to 350°F.

In a mixer fitted with the paddle attachment, combine the flour and butter until the butter is completely mixed with the flour and the mixture has a sandy appearance. Drizzle in the ice water until the mixture comes together.

Divide dough in to three equal pieces. With a pasta roller or by hand with a rolling pin, roll each piece into a sheet about 5 inches wide by 12 to 18 inches long. Place on individual baking sheets. Sprinkle the salt evenly over the dough sheets and bake until crisp and light brown, about 30 minutes. Let cool, then break into random shapes.

MAKES ABOUT THREE 5 BY 18-INCH SHEETS OF CRACKERS

3½ cups unbleached all-purpose flour

2 sticks (16 tablespoons) unsalted butter

¾ cup ice water

1½ tablespoons sea salt

Cornbread with Maple Butter

You can bake this in a 12-inch cast-iron skillet, a 12 by 12-inch pan, or a 12-cup muffin tin.

If using a convection oven, preheat to 375°F and turn on the convection fan; if using a standard oven, cook at 385°F. Grease a 12-inch cast-iron skillet (or pan or muffin tin) with butter and place the pan in the oven to preheat for about 6 minutes.

Meanwhile, mix the batter: In a medium bowl, combine the flour, sugar, cornmeal, baking powder, and salt. In a large bowl, whisk together the eggs, buttermilk, and oil. Add the dry ingredients to the wet ingredients and stir until well combined. Remove the heated pan from the oven and pour the batter into it. Bake for 15 minutes. Test for doneness by inserting a cake tester or paring knife into the center; it should come out clean. Let the cornbread cool completely in the pan.

Remove the cornbread from the pan, slice into wedges or squares, and serve with maple butter.

MAKES ABOUT 12 SERVINGS

Unsalted butter for greasing the skillet or pan

2½ cups unbleached all-purpose flour

¾ cup sugar

1 cup cornmeal

2 tablespoons baking powder

2 teaspoons kosher salt

3 large eggs

1 cup buttermilk

¼ cup corn oil

8 ounces Maple Butter (page 227)

Buttermilk Biscuits

MAKES 16 BISCUITS

4½ cups unbleached all-purpose flour, plus more for the surface

2 tablespoons kosher salt

3 tablespoons sugar

¼ cup baking powder

2 sticks (16 tablespoons) unsalted butter, cold

1¾ cups plus 3 tablespoons buttermilk

This is a great biscuit recipe, but success depends on the mixing of the dough. It should all be done by hand and mixed just long enough that everything comes together. Do not overwork the dough. After the dough has been cut, you can easily freeze the biscuits raw. Place frozen biscuits directly in the oven and bake them without thawing them first.

Preheat the oven to 400°F. If you have a convection oven, turn on the convection fan.

In a medium bowl, mix together the flour, salt, sugar, and baking powder. Using a box grater, grate the butter on the largest holes into the dry ingredients and then use your fingers to rub the butter into the dry mixture so it is well combined, with some flecks of butter remaining visible. Create a well in the dry mixture and pour in 1¾ cups buttermilk. With a rubber spatula, fold in the buttermilk until the mixture begins to form a dough. Place the dough on a lightly floured surface and knead by hand just until the buttermilk is completely incorporated. Be careful not to overmix the dough.

Press the dough into an 8 by 8-inch square about 2 inches thick. Trim the edges to make them even, then cut the dough into 4 by 4-inch squares. Transfer the squares to a baking sheet. Brush the tops with the remaining buttermilk and bake for 9 minutes. Rotate the baking sheet, then bake for another 9 minutes.

A Trio of Pestos

Basil pesto should be in your refrigerator all summer. Don't be afraid to freeze it in small batches and pull it out as you need it. Add other herbs or arugula for great flavor options. I've included recipes for cilantro and walnut pestos, variations that have great applications.

Basil Pesto

Place the basil, pine nuts, Parmesan, and garlic in the bowl of a food processor fitted with a metal blade. Pulse until everything comes together. With the machine running, add the olive oil through the tube in a thin stream and process until the mixture is well blended and the oil is fully incorporated; you may need to scrape down the sides of the bowl once to fully combine. Season with salt and pepper and refrigerate for up to 3 to 4 days.

Cilantro Pesto

Place the herbs, pine nuts, garlic, jalapeño, and lime zest in a blender. With the blender running, add the olive oil in a thin stream. Blend until smooth. Season with salt and pepper. Refrigerate for up to 3 to 4 days.

Walnut Pesto

Place the toasted walnuts in the bowl of a food processor fitted with the metal blade and pulse until the walnuts are chopped into small pieces. Add the garlic, Parmesan, olive oil, and lemon zest and puree until everything is combined. Season with salt and pepper. Use immediately or refrigerate for up to 1 week.

FOR THE BASIL PESTO

MAKES ABOUT 1 CUP

2 cups tightly packed basil leaves

3 tablespoons pine nuts, toasted

¼ cup grated Parmesan

2 cloves garlic

⅔ cup extra-virgin olive oil

Kosher salt and freshly ground black pepper

FOR THE CILANTRO PESTO

MAKES ABOUT 1 CUP

1 cup tightly packed cilantro leaves (some stem attached is okay)

½ cup flat-leaf parsley leaves

3 tablespoons pine nuts, lightly toasted

2 cloves garlic

1 small jalapeño, halved and seeded

Finely grated zest of 1 lime

½ cup extra-virgin olive oil

Kosher salt and freshly ground black pepper

FOR THE WALNUT PESTO

MAKES ABOUT 1 CUP

½ cup walnuts, lightly toasted

1 clove garlic

3 tablespoons grated Parmesan

¼ cup extra-virgin olive oil

½ teaspoon finely grated lemon zest

Kosher salt and freshly ground black pepper

Aïoli

MAKES ABOUT 1 CUP

2 egg yolks

2 cloves garlic

1 tablespoon freshly squeezed
  lemon juice

1 tablespoon champagne vinegar

2 teaspoons Dijon mustard

½ cup extra-virgin olive oil

½ cup canola oil

Kosher salt and freshly ground
  black pepper

This is a basic sauce, but an important one that can play a versatile role in so many recipes. We serve aïoli with a lot of fried seafood, but it is also a starting point for many variations. It can easily be turned into a great tartar sauce or enhanced with herbs and seasonings. It can be sweet, spicy, earthy, or umami-flavored. At the restaurants, we always have plenty of good aïoli on hand.

In a food processor fitted with the metal blade, puree the yolks, garlic, lemon juice, vinegar, and mustard until combined. Scrape the sides down with a rubber spatula and pulse a few more times to make sure the ingredients are well blended. With the food processor running, slowly add the oils in a thin stream through the tube and let them emulsify with the yolks. If the mixture becomes too thick, add a few drops of cold water—you shouldn't need more than 1 tablespoon—and continue adding the oil. The finished aïoli should easily coat a spoon. Season with salt and pepper. Refrigerate in an airtight container for up to 5 days.

AÏOLI VARIATIONS

Mayonnaise: Omit the garlic.

Horseradish Mayonnaise or Aïoli: Add 2 tablespoons prepared horseradish, 2 teaspoons Worcestershire sauce, and 1 tablespoon Tabasco sauce to the aïoli or mayonnaise recipe.

Tartar Sauce: Fold in 3 tablespoons minced dill pickles, 3 tablespoons minced red onion, 2 tablespoons rinsed, drained, and chopped capers, and 1 tablespoon chopped fresh flat-leaf parsley leaves. You can make this with either aïoli or mayonnaise.

Tomato Aïoli: Omit the vinegar. Wash, core, and chop 2 vine-ripened red tomatoes for about 1½ cups. Place the tomatoes in a medium nonstick skillet and simmer over medium heat, stirring frequently, until cooked down to about ½ cup. Allow the tomatoes to cool. Add to the food processor with the yolks, garlic, lemon juice, and mustard. Follow the recipe from there.

Malt Vinegar Aïoli: Replace the lemon juice and champagne vinegar with 2 tablespoons good-quality malt vinegar.

Spicy Aïoli: Omit the lemon juice and champagne vinegar. Add 2 tablespoons freshly squeezed lime juice and 2 tablespoons sriracha hot sauce.

Black Garlic Aïoli: Black garlic is fermented garlic; it can be bought in specialty stores as a head of garlic or as individual cloves. Replace the regular garlic in the aïoli recipe with 6 cloves of black garlic.

Togarashi Aïoli: Replace the lemon juice with 2 tablespoons orange juice and add 1 tablespoon togarashi spice.

Grain Mustard Aïoli: Replace the Dijon mustard with 2 tablespoons whole grain mustard.

Lemon Aïoli: Add the zest and juice of 1 whole lemon.

Beurre Blanc

Once you master this classic sauce you can adapt it endlessly by adding fresh herbs, dry spices, or shrimp shells to the reduction.

Combine the shallot, bay leaf, thyme, peppercorns, vinegar, and wine in a medium saucepan and place over medium-low heat. Simmer gently until the liquid is reduced to about 2 tablespoons. Increase the heat to medium and whisk in 2 cubes of the butter. Continue whisking briskly until the butter is almost completely melted. Add the remaining butter pieces one at a time, whisking and allowing each to melt before adding more. Do not let the sauce come to a simmer or it will break. If the sauce starts to simmer, remove the pan from the heat and continue whisking in the butter off the heat.

After all of the butter has been added, strain the sauce through a fine-mesh strainer and season with salt and pepper. Add the dill, if using. The sauce must be kept warm at a consistent temperature until you are ready to use it; never let it boil or simmer as it will break the sauce.

MAKES ABOUT 1 CUP

1 small shallot, minced

1 bay leaf

1 sprig thyme

3 whole black peppercorns

¼ cup white wine vinegar

½ cup dry white wine

3 sticks (24 tablespoons) unsalted butter, cold, cut into 1-inch cubes

Kosher salt and freshly ground black pepper

1 tablespoon chopped dill (optional)

Compound Butters

These butters add so much to a dish. I've included a few simple flavors that are classic with many seafoods. Don't use so much butter that it melts all over the plate. You want just enough to top the dish—a little goes a long way. Wrap the butter in plastic wrap, shape it into a cylinder, refrigerate it, then slice off a little as you need it. These butters will keep for a few weeks in the refrigerator and a few months in the freezer.

FOR THE HORSERADISH BUTTER

MAKES ONE 8-INCH CYLINDER,
12 TO 16 SLICES

1½ sticks (12 tablespoons) unsalted butter at room temperature

1 tablespoon prepared horseradish

2 tablespoons chopped flat-leaf parsley leaves

2 tablespoons panko breadcrumbs

½ teaspoon Tabasco sauce

½ teaspoon finely grated lemon zest

Horseradish Butter

Combine all ingredients in a food processor fitted with a metal blade and process until smooth. Using plastic wrap, roll the butter into a 2-inch-diameter cylinder about 8 inches long and wrap tightly. Refrigerate until ready to use.

FOR THE PARSLEY BUTTER

MAKES ONE 12-INCH CYLINDER,
18 TO 20 SLICES

4 sticks (1 pound) unsalted butter at room temperature

2 cups tightly packed flat-leaf parsley leaves

Parsley Butter

Place all ingredients in a food processor fitted with the metal blade and process until smooth. Using plastic wrap, roll the butter into a 2-inch-diameter cylinder and wrap tightly. Refrigerate until ready to use.

FOR THE LEMON-GARLIC BUTTER

MAKES ONE 12-INCH CYLINDER,
18 TO 20 SLICES

1½ cups canola oil

12 cloves garlic

4 sticks (1 pound) unsalted butter at room temperature

Finely grated zest and juice of 1 lemon

Lemon-Garlic Butter

Chef's note: This recipe makes about 2 cups confit garlic when you only need 2 tablespoons, but you will find plenty of other uses for it.

Place the canola oil and garlic in a small saucepan. Heat over medium-high heat until it begins to bubble. Reduce the heat to medium-low and simmer for 3 minutes. Remove the pan from the heat and let the garlic cool to room temperature in the oil. The garlic should not be too dark but should be soft and spreadable all the way through. Pour the oil and garlic into an airtight container, making sure the oil covers the garlic completely, and refrigerate. For the butter, combine the butter, lemon zest and juice, and 2 tablespoons of the confit garlic cloves in a food processor fitted with the metal blade and puree until smooth. Using plastic wrap, roll the butter into a 2-inch-diameter cylinder and wrap tightly. Refrigerate until ready to use.

Smoked Uni Butter

In a food processor fitted with a metal blade, combine the uni and butter and process until smooth. Scrape the butter onto a piece of plastic wrap and shape into a 2-inch-diameter cylinder. Refrigerate until ready to use.

Anchovy Butter

Place all ingredients in a food processor fitted with the metal blade and process until smooth. Using plastic wrap, roll the butter into a 2-inch-diameter cylinder and wrap tightly. Refrigerate until ready to use.

Maple Butter

In a stand mixer fitted with the paddle attachment, whip the butter on low for 3 minutes. Add the maple syrup in a thin stream and whip until it is completely incorporated into the butter. Add the salt and mix 1 to 2 additional minutes. Transfer to a container with a tight-fitting lid. Serve at room temperature.

FOR THE SMOKED UNI BUTTER

MAKES ONE 12-INCH CYLINDER, 18 TO 20 SLICES

2 ounces Smoked Uni (page 62)

4 sticks (1 pound) unsalted butter at room temperature

FOR THE ANCHOVY BUTTER

MAKES ONE 8-INCH CYLINDER, 12 TO 16 SLICES

1½ sticks (12 tablespoons) unsalted butter at room temperature

1 or 2 anchovy filets, about 1 ounce, rinsed and drained

1 teaspoon chopped tarragon

1 teaspoon chopped dill

1 teaspoon finely grated lemon zest

¼ teaspoon ground turmeric

½ teaspoon kosher salt

¼ teaspoon ground white pepper

FOR THE MAPLE BUTTER

MAKES ABOUT 1 CUP

2 sticks (16 tablespoons) unsalted butter at room temperature

½ cup maple syrup

1 teaspoon kosher salt

Harissa Vinaigrette

MAKES ABOUT 1 CUP

3 tablespoons harissa paste

2 tablespoons red wine vinegar

1 tablespoon honey

½ teaspoon finely grated lemon zest

1 small roasted shallot

¾ cup extra-virgin olive oil

Kosher salt

Harissa is a North African blend of peppers and spices that adds a pop of flavor to sauces and vinaigrettes. A little of this bold, zippy seasoning goes a long way. One of my favorite simple snacks is cucumber sticks dipped in this tangy vinaigrette. Unless you have the oven on for another purpose, roast the shallot in a toaster oven until soft.

Place the harissa paste, vinegar, honey, lemon zest, and shallot in a blender and puree. With the blender running, add the oil through the tube in a thin stream and puree until blended together. Season with salt.

Ginger Vinegar

MAKES ABOUT 1 CUP

One 4-inch knob ginger, peeled and chopped

¾ cup white wine vinegar

½ cup sugar

This is a great addition to crudos, tartares, and seafood right off the grill.

Place all ingredients in a small saucepan and bring to a boil. Reduce to a simmer and cook for 10 minutes. Remove the pan from the heat and let the mixture sit until it reaches room temperature.

Strain and refrigerate. Ginger vinegar will keep for up to 3 weeks.

Tempura Batter

This is a simple batter that is great for fish and vegetables. It's best used on items that are cut small; you don't want to use this on a large piece of fish. The batter should be thick enough to coat your finger but still drip off, somewhere between pancake batter and cream.

In a medium bowl, stir together the flours, cornstarch, baking soda, and salt. Whisking constantly, add the sparkling water in a thin stream until the batter reaches the desired consistency. Use immediately or refrigerate for up to 5 hours. Just before using, thoroughly whisk the batter.

MAKES ABOUT 2 CUPS

½ cup unbleached all-purpose flour

¼ cup rice flour

¼ cup cornstarch

2 teaspoons baking soda

1 teaspoon kosher salt

About 1 cup sparkling water

Seasoned Flour

I use this flour to coat most types of fish and shellfish for frying. It's flavorful but not overpowering, so it doesn't compete with the more subtle flavors of seafood.

Combine all ingredients and stir together. Store in an airtight container at room temperature for up to 1 month.

MAKES ABOUT 3½ CUPS

2 cups unbleached all-purpose flour

1 cup rice flour

½ cup corn flour

2 teaspoons paprika

2 teaspoons dry mustard

½ teaspoon cayenne pepper

1 teaspoon onion powder

1 teaspoon kosher salt

½ teaspoon freshly ground black pepper

Fish Stock

MAKES ABOUT 1 QUART

1 pound white-fleshed fish bones, rinsed

½ cup sliced button mushrooms

¼ cup chopped celery

¼ cup chopped leek

½ cup chopped yellow onion

6 whole black peppercorns

2 bay leaves

2 sprigs thyme

½ cup dry white wine

1 sprig flat-leaf parsley

½ lemon

There is nothing fishy about fish stock. When made well, it's a fantastic addition to your cooking arsenal. This is a classic element of many soups and sauces, especially those served with seafood. And it's a great way to utilize any extra fish pieces and bits left over after buying and butchering a whole fish. Always use the bones of mild, white-fleshed fish like cod, haddock, flounder, or halibut. If using the heads, be sure to remove the gills. For something different, you could lightly cold-smoke the bones before making the stock.

Place all ingredients in a large stockpot and add cold water to cover. Bring to a boil and then quickly reduce to a simmer. Let simmer for 25 minutes. Turn off the heat and let the mixture sit for 30 minutes. Set a strainer over a large bowl. Strain the stock by ladling it out of the pot and into the strainer. Let the last inch or so remain in the pot; this will ensure a clear stock.

Let the stock cool and store in airtight containers in the refrigerator or freeze in small batches. The stock will keep 2 to 3 days in the refrigerator or in the freezer for up to 1 month.

Vegetable Stock

MAKES ABOUT 2 QUARTS

½ cup chopped yellow onion

¼ cup chopped celery

¼ cup chopped carrot

¼ cup chopped fennel

3 large button mushrooms, sliced

1 wedge orange

1 sprig thyme

1 bay leaf

5 whole black peppercorns

You should always have a batch of vegetable stock in your refrigerator or freezer. Use it in place of water when cooking grains, rice, and beans for an added layer of flavor.

Place all ingredients in a large stockpot and add 2 quarts of water. Bring to a boil, then reduce to a simmer and let simmer for 20 minutes. Remove from the heat and let cool to room temperature. Strain and discard the solids.

Store in an airtight container in the refrigerator for 7 days or in the freezer for up to 2 months.

Mushroom Stock

This is another staple that can be used for a variety of dishes. For a deeper flavor, replace the water with Vegetable Stock (opposite).

In a large saucepan, heat the canola oil over medium heat and add the mushrooms, onion, celery, and garlic. Cook the vegetables until they begin to brown. Add 2½ cups water, the bay leaf, thyme, and peppercorns. Bring to a simmer and continue simmering for 20 minutes. Remove from the heat and let cool to room temperature.

Strain into an airtight container and refrigerate for up to 7 days, or freeze for up to 2 months.

MAKES 2 CUPS

2 tablespoons canola oil

2 cups sliced button mushrooms

½ cup chopped yellow onion

¼ cup chopped celery

2 cloves garlic, chopped

1 bay leaf

2 sprigs thyme

5 black peppercorns

Lobster Stock

If you're cooking lobsters at home, you may as well make your own lobster stock with the bodies. It might sound daunting, but it's actually easy to do. You can use this stock as a base for soups and stews or to cook lentils. Remove the outer shells from the bodies and clean away the insides, making sure to scrape away the gills. Leave the legs attached to the body shell, since they add an extra layer of flavor.

Preheat the oven to 400°F.

Place the lobster shells in a roasting pan and roast until the shells have browned lightly, 10 to 15 minutes. Remove and set aside.

In a large saucepan, heat the canola oil over medium heat. Add the onion, celery, and carrot and cook until lightly colored. Add the tomato and tomato paste and continue cooking until the ingredients are thoroughly combined. Add the lobster shells and white wine and bring the mixture to a boil.

Add enough cold water to the pan to cover the lobster shells and bring the mixture back to a boil. Once it is boiling, add the thyme, bay leaves, and peppercorns. Lower the heat and simmer for 30 minutes. Remove the pan from the heat and let it sit for 30 minutes.

Strain the stock into an airtight container and cool to room temperature. Refrigerate for 4 to 5 days or freeze for up to 2 months.

MAKES ABOUT 1 QUART

4 lobster shells, cleaned

3 tablespoons canola oil

1 cup chopped yellow onion

¼ cup chopped celery

¼ cup chopped carrot

¼ cup chopped tomato

1 tablespoon tomato paste

1 cup dry white wine

2 sprigs thyme

2 bay leaves

5 whole black peppercorns

RESOURCES

Having a great oyster bar (or just recreating your own at home) starts with connecting with the important people who supply our seafood. From the most seasoned and experienced farmers, like Skip Bennett (Island Creek Oysters), Adam James (Hama Hama Oysters), and John Finger (Hog Island Oyster Co.), to newcomers like Conor Walsh and Russ Hilliard (Swell Oyster Co.), oyster farmers share a dedication, work ethic, and passion that's hard to match. If you get a chance to visit any of these farms and eat their oysters in person, you should. If you can get over to the 100-plus-year-old Boston Fish Pier and pick up seafood from Red's Best, I highly encourage that, too. And if you can't, most of these sources are happy to ship their product to you. For everything else, find your local people—the farmers at the markets and farm stands, the fishermen, the butchers—as they will help the recipes in this cookbook come alive.

Hama Hama Oysters, Lilliwaup, Washington
(360) 877-5811
hamahamaoysters.com
Washington State oysters and clams

Hog Island Oyster Co., Marshall, California
(415) 663-9218
hogislandoysters.com
Northern California oysters and other shellfish

Island Creek Oysters, Duxbury, Massachusetts
(781) 934-2028
islandcreekoysters.com
Oysters, caviar, and so much more

The Maine Oyster Company, Portland, Maine
(207) 956-0147
themaineoystercompany.com
Maine oysters

Red's Best, Boston, Massachusetts
(617) 830-1672
redsbest.com
Wide variety of fish and shellfish

Swell Oyster Co., Hampton, New Hampshire
(603) 498-1938
swelloysterco.com
New Hampshire oysters

ACKNOWLEDGMENTS

Even in this uncertain time I feel very fortunate. Restaurant life seemed to change overnight when the pandemic hit, and few of us were ready to handle the effects of Covid-19 on our industry. But I have been blessed to have amazing people around me to help me stumble through this moment.

For this project, first of all, I am grateful to Sandy Gilbert and the team at Rizzoli—Sandy's encouragement allowed me and my coauthor, Erin, to move forward with this project in spite of everything. I'm thankful for the patience she showed as we took our time to figure out how to get this cookbook made in all the right ways.

I am so thankful to the entire staff at our restaurants. When things were great, they gave 100 percent. And when things were hard, they seemed to give more, even in the face of impossible circumstances. That also goes for my business partner, Shore Gregory, who has been a rock and a steady hand for all of us. Shore is a great friend and I look forward to a long future in this industry together.

To our many employees, past and present: I am so glad to know you all. There are too many to mention but here are a few: the Erins, Krista, Molly W., Niki T., Nate, Val, Dora, Susie, Van, Laura, Meg, Craig, Aldamar, Astrid, Issac, Chelsea, Ryan, Ally, James, Matty, Ashley, Rob, Fran, Katie, Phil, Bobby, and Jimmy. Special shout-out to Nicola Hobson, thank you for ten-plus years of being an incredible chef.

To Bill Weiss and the incredible crew at Island Creek Oysters: Thank you for all of your education and for finding us the best oysters.

To the fishermen, farmers, and purveyors who provide their products to our families and guests every day—my sincerest gratitude. Especially to Mark Sewall: I love telling anyone who will listen that my cousin catches all of our lobster. And thanks to Michael Chambers and Gunnar Ek for teaching me so much about responsible aquaculture.

To all my recipe testers and helpers, I am amazed and thankful that we got this done in such a crazy time. Claudia and Meredith, your testing and feedback were essential. Catrine Kelty, our food stylist, you made everything look so beautiful, and Harrison Grant, thank you for your photo assistant skills.

George Restrepo and Lisa Diercks at Endpaper Studio: Thank you for your work and talent bringing all of these elements to life.

To Erin Byers Murray and Michael Harlan Turkell, who are my great friends and the most indispensable book partners: I'm always grateful to work with you both.

I have to thank my family for always being wonderful: Lisa, Hudson, Ethan, and Sophia. I love that we got extra time together during this whole thing and can't wait until we can go out into the world again. Thank you to my sisters, Jennifer, Mary, and Amanda, who are always supportive. And to the Grants, thank you for being such great neighbors and eaters during this project. And Gethin, thank you for all the years of support and friendship.

One of the wonderful things that came out of this horrible moment in time was that my son Hudson came home from college early and that gave us the opportunity to spend time together, including a few months working at the restaurant side by side. Because Hudson is the oldest son, during his youngest years I was in the kitchen. Like too many of us who work in kitchens, I ended up missing a lot. But I have loved every second of this moment, of getting to drive to and from work with him and spending the day teaching him all I could. He was here in the early, dark days of being shut down, when we were forced to shrink to a small team and did take out, and he

was a big part of that team. I feel lucky to have found that special time with him.

I am hopeful for the future. I know that food will continue to shape my life and the lives of so many around me. Be appreciative of one another. And eat more seafood.

—*Jeremy Sewall*

When we set out on this project years ago, the word pandemic never crossed our minds. But in spring 2020, when we were not quite halfway finished with this book, the world stopped. Suddenly Jeremy was facing restaurant closures, staff layoffs, and total uncertainty about his own future. Could we really push forward and finish a book right now? After a few long conversations, Jeremy made the call—we would finish strong. I will always be grateful for his perseverance, his humor, and, of course, his vision. Thank you for letting me be a part of your cookbook journey once again, Chef.

To our team, Sandy, George, Lisa, Michael, Catrine, Claudia, Natalie—thank you for sticking by us and for sharing your knowledge, talents, and gifts to make this book real.

I wouldn't have made it through this crazy time, or this project, without my family's endless support, and especially their laughter. Dave, Charlie, and Maggie, you guys make life delicious every single day.

—*Erin Byers Murray*

First published in the United States of America in 2021 by
Rizzoli International Publications, Inc.
300 Park Avenue South
New York, NY 10010
www.rizzoliusa.com

Text copyright © 2021 Erin Byers Murray and Jeremy Sewall
Recipes copyright © 2021 Jeremy Sewall
Photography copyright © 2021 Michael Harlan Turkell with the exception of
pages 7 Eva Kolenko and 233 Emily Dorio

Publisher: Charles Miers
Project Editor: Sandra Gilbert Freidus
Design: Lisa Diercks and George Restrepo / Endpaper Studio
Production Manager: Alyn Evans
Managing Editor: Lynn Scrabis
Food Styling: Catrine Kelty
Additional Editorial: Natalie Danford, Tricia Levi

All rights reserved. No part of this publication may be reproduced, stored in
a retrieval system, or transmitted in any form or by any means, electronic,
mechanical, photocopying, recording, or otherwise, without prior consent of
the publishers.

Printed in China

2021 2022 2023 2024 / 10 9 8 7 6 5 4 3 2 1

ISBN 978-0-8478-6983-1
Library of Congress Control Number: 2021937245

Visit us online:
Facebook.com/RizzoliNewYork
instagram.com/rizzolibooks
twitter.com/Rizzoli_Books
pinterest.com/rizzolibooks
youtube.com/user/RizzoliNY
issuu.com/Rizzoli

The acclaimed Boston restaurants of CHEF JEREMY SEWALL, Island Creek Oyster Bar and Row 34, have received praise in the *New York Times* and *Bon Appétit*. He is the author of the James Beard–nominated Rizzoli cookbook *The New England Kitchen: Fresh Takes on Seasonal Recipes*.

ERIN BYERS MURRAY is a journalist specializing in food and wine, and author of food books including *Shucked: Life on a New England Oyster Farm* and *Grits: A Cultural & Culinary Journey Through the South*.

James Beard award-winner CHEF RENEE ERICKSON runs several Seattle restaurants, including the Walrus and the Carpenter.

Food photographer and author MICHAEL HARLAN TURKELL's work has appeared in numerous publications. His cookbooks include *Acid Trip: Travels in the World of Vinegar*.